THE TEN COMMANDMENTS OF PREACHING

C.L. LAWRENCE

Fallon House Publishers, LLC
New Jersey

DEDICATED TO

The Rev. Dr. Donald Sullivan Medley

THE TEN COMMANDMENTS
OF PREACHING

CONTENTS

ACKNOWLEDGMENTS

Two women of God whose presence of poise, grace and elegance in the pulpit is eclipsed only by their powerfully anointed preaching.

Rev. Dr. Prathia L. Hall (January 1, 1940 – August 12, 2002), leader and activist in the Civil Rights Movement, womanist theologian, and ethicist. The Elijah in my life, who taught me to go beyond "flat reading," walk circumspectly between the lines of the text to see the unseen; and to ask God for the voice of the people. She opened my eyes to a boundless world view that finds relevance and reason in the Word in any context. I honor and cherish the memory of her mother love, as sister/friend and unselfish mentorship that influenced my life and ministry beyond measure.

Bishop, Dr. Millicent H. Hunter, Sr. Pastor of the Baptist Worship Center Church, Philadelphia, PA and Presiding Prelate of the Worship Center World Wide Fellowship of Churches. Her example of relentless commitment and unquestioning obedience to God has shown me the endless possibilities of God's purpose for those who dare to believe for more. When they said, she shouldn't, she pursued. When they said, she couldn't, she did. Beneath the weight of every test and trial, disappointment, and setback, through struggles and pain, she embodied Maya Angelou's "Still I Rise."

INTRODUCTION

Since this isn't a commentary on the Ten Commandments that Moses brought down on tablets of stone from Mt. Sinai, or a "how to" on preaching them, the obvious question might be, "Then what does this book have to do with preaching?" It has everything to do with preaching. There are six entities involved in preaching, (1) God, the Father, (2) God, the Son, Jesus, (3) God, the Holy Spirit, (4) the written Word of God, (5) the hearer, and (6) the preacher, the vessel. No one would argue the supremacy and divine authority of the first four, the Divine Entities; or the importance of the fifth, the people. While this book acknowledges each, the passionate concern of this writing is for the person of the preacher. The preacher is expected to be a finally tuned vessel through whom living waters flow; able to meet the intellectual expectations of homiletics, hermeneutics, astutely interpret the integration of culture and Word, while staying humble in the unspoken impact of pulpit presence. All of that is a part of preaching so this book has everything to do with preaching.

I pastored a church in the early 2000s. After about three months I found out the true story of the well-guarded secret of my predecessor's departure. Suicide. There's much that could be read into the details but the point is, he took his life. A man of God, pastor of a respected church, took his life. That experience heightened my passionate concern for the dynamics within and around "the person of the preacher." The preacher as a person gets little attention until scandal erupts, or the high rate of suicide among preachers gets noticed, or an article is written about the mass exit of clergy back into the secular workforce. All after the fact. What about nuances that matter but overlooked because, shall we say, the tyranny of the urgent.

OK! There you are! Called to preach, uniquely gifted, anointed, armed and fully clad in the whole armor of God. Seminary behind you, visions before you, Bible apps on all your smart devices. Have Sermon Will Travel! Ready to preach in season and out of season. But wait! There are a few things you need to know before you go; things they don't tell you in seminary or Bible institutes. As a preacher, you may be in positions other than pastor, but you're still perceived as a leader. Though differing across denominations and culture, there're certain perceptions and responsibilities that come with the call. You'll learn as you go but OJT (On the Job Training), as in the secular arena, has limitations. Mistakes are costly, and sad as it is, sometimes unforgiven. You would be wise to learn from the experience of seasoned others who desire your highest good.

The Ten Commandments of Preaching is a canon of fundamental ethical principles invaluable to preachers at every level of experience. Excellence doesn't happen by prayer alone but by the deliberate embrace and continued practice of precepts that prepare and position you to be exalted by the Holy Spirit in your due season. The powerful principles I share in the following pages aren't secrets, but overlooked and often underestimated tenets that can shape, perfect and sustain you throughout your ministerial journey.

In the Hollywood movie, The Ten Commandments,[a] Moses, portrayed by Charlton Heston, came down from Mt.

---

[a] The Ten Commandments 1956 epic film produced and directed by Cecil B. DeMille

Sinai, hair white, face aglow, the Ten Commandments etched on two tablets of stone braced in his arms, saying he'd been in the presence of God. Today The Ten Commandments of Preaching can be downloaded to your handheld devices, or bound between the cover of a book. Your hair, probably, won't turn white and without the aid of cosmetics you'll probably not have that "Moses glow" depicted in the movie. But, if in the pursuit of excellence, you internalize The Ten Commandments of Preaching, you'll glow with God's favor as you excel beyond the level of mediocrity in your call to preach the Good News in the Word of God.

I wrote The Ten Commandments of Preaching because you asked me to. After every leadership seminar, conference, and training session, I'd prayerfully ponder the thoughts and questions shared, hoping I'd added meaningful value beyond that of a great learning experience. Finally, there was an undeniable God breathed voice in my spirit, "You have your assignment, just do it."

Nurture your mind with great thoughts, for you will never go any higher than you think.

— Benjamin Disrael

THE 1ST COMMANDMENT

THOU SHALL KEEP THY HEAD ON STRAIGHT

EXCITING. INTIMIDATING. OVERWHELMING. Fearful. Unqualified. Ready, Oh, no! Not ready. How will this change my life? How will this affect my family? Will people approve and support me? ... A myriad of thoughts and emotions associated with the realization of the call on your life to preach the Good News of Jesus Christ. All legitimate feelings, different for everyone. Some run from the call. Others step up with enthusiasm. There is no right or wrong reaction. Your response to the call is largely reflective of your understanding of "call," your personality, the way you accept challenges, and how you view the ministry in general and preaching in particular. If you come from a long line of preachers in your family, then you (should) know what you're getting into. Others, perhaps first in their family to be called, know nothing beyond what they see on Sunday mornings, TV, YouTube or streaming on the net. They certainly know nothing about being a preacher and the life that comes with it. Everyone works through the maze of emotions and thought processes in their own way. There are, however, some things of common concern to every preacher – or should be. Keeping your head on straight is one of them.

The call to preach is infinitely more than crafting and delivering a "good" sermon. Although that's important, if your head isn't on straight you'll tarnish the dignity of the call and diminish the hallowed efficacy of even your best sermon. Keeping your head on straight is a system of self-governance and self-control by means of the best use of the wisdom and understanding available. Keeping your head on straight is inclusive of a host of dynamics, responsibilities and challenges that are revealed along the way. It's keeping your eye on the ball, staying focused and avoiding distractions. It's being down-to-earth relative to self-perception and how you see others. It means to think clearly and make good decisions that will have future benefit.[b] It means being realistic about your vision for yourself and how to get there. Having your head on straight is being aware of your priorities and what's expedient.[c] Keeping your head on straight is an assignment: trying to walk worthy of the call, honoring God with your best in study and delivery, managing the dynamics that come with the high visibility innate in the call, meeting the demands of life (family, work), voices clamoring about this and that and everything in between, and still you must stay grounded. No matter how high your star rises, keeping your head on straight is always your "in the moment" assignment.

> Keeping your head on straight is a perpetual "in the moment" assignment

I beseech you, therefore, my brothers and sisters, by the mercies of God, that you do not underestimate the importance of this first commandment, for to violate the first commandment at any point in your ministry can be your undoing. It's not an easy task. The call to preach is a call to a ministry in which high visibility just comes with the call; it comes with the terrain. Unless you're preaching ministry is restricted to terrestrial or

---

[b] Galatians 6:7
[c] I Corinthians 6:12

internet radio, you're highly visible. During the sermon, everyone sees you but you don't see everyone. More people know you than the other way around. And, however awesome you are, at the beginning, middle and end of the day you're human and subject to human fragilities. Always be aware of that. You'll need to find ways to keep yourself grounded because a preacher is an easy mark for sins that fall into the three categories: Lust of the Flesh, Lust of the Eye, and Pride of Life. In addition to having to resist the temptations which emanate from within, because of the visibility factor, you must also contend with the same sins of which you are targeted by others.

While you can't control the motives of others, neither their feelings or intentions, you can control outcomes to the extent to which you're able to control yourself. Having the right perspective of God, the call and yourself is the place to begin. Again, understand that the call to preach is more than sermon delivery. Once you get a rhythm with the Holy Spirit, a handle on homiletics and hermeneutics, your voice, your style, sermon delivery is the easy part of the call. The concern of this first commandment, is helping you get and keep the right perspective so that you will stay grounded as you serve in the high calling of preaching the Good News of Jesus Christ.

There's no human logic as to whom God calls to preach. Some preachers are naturally charismatic orators. Some have a commanding pulpit presence. Some have the gift of storytelling. Others may have the intellect to more easily understand and integrate the scholarly material. Some come from a long generational line of preachers, while another is the first in generations to even go to church. The call truly rests in the explanation found in I Corinthians 12,[d] wherein it explains that the Spirit of God distributes spiritual gifts just as he decides. God does it this way so that we don't think there's something about us that sets us apart and qualifies us above others to preach

---

[d] I Corinthians 12:11

the Gospel. You can talk about what this one has and that one doesn't but the conversation is short lived because no real common denominator can be found aside from being a child of the Most High God.

The most unlikely person in our eyes may be the pastor of a mega church with strong active worldwide ministries while another who seems to have all the" right stuff" is pastoring a church whose growth has stagnated for years at less than 100 members. In some cases, we may be able to see what stunts the ministry of some preachers and we'll touch on that in later commandments, but realistically speaking we just don't know the mind of God when it comes to how he decides whom he calls. We can see there are many facets of the call but we can't see the prerequisites from God's point of view.

While God does call the human vessel to preach the Gospel, the ministry of preaching is bigger than any person. If there were a window through which one could look onto the vast landscape of preaching, you'd see a world bigger than any congregation you could ever imagine. You'd see broken, hurting, and discouraged people looking for hope; vibrant, energetic people full of dreams yet in need of direction; community leaders, CEOs, managers, people in high places, people of low estate, in need of strength and encouragement that only God can give. The common denominator at all levels in any society is people. Never lose sight of the people and your purpose among them.[e] The call to preach is predicated upon a relationship; your relationship with Jesus. A love relationship. That's big.

When Jesus and Peter were talking in John 21, Jesus upset the flow of the conversation when he threw love in the mix. He asked Peter three times if he loved him. Peter rather stumbled with his response to the question. Maybe the subject of love was unexpected. Peter was a "dude," a grassroots fisherman. Maybe his "macho" was uncomfortable with the

---

[e] John 21:15, 16, 17

emotional spin on the conversation. Nevertheless, Jesus was making it clear that a relationship with him was more than just being around him.

He had followers everywhere he went. Jesus was really the first "celebrity preacher." There's no depth to some followers. Some are there just to be there with no idea why, just there because that's where the crowd is moving. Some only want to say they were in the place. Some follow out of a sense of curiosity. Others for the fish and the loaves. Jesus was taking it to the level of where the rubber meets the road. Jesus knew that if you put a condition or a qualifier on a relationship, you'll see who's with you when the sun comes up. He said, effectively, "You're here but do you love me? If you love me then you will do what matters to me. He made a direct connection between love for him and taking care of what was his. "If you love me, then feed my sheep. If you love me then feed my lambs." You can't love Jesus and do nothing. If you love Jesus you have to do what matters to him, and in the way he would do it. Jesus was passing his mantle, the monumental task of loving and caring for the sheep to Peter.

Never lose sight of the people or your purpose among them

Preaching, therefore, is a ministry of feeding, providing life giving and life sustaining sustenance to the human sheep and lambs. Preaching the Word of God is a divine trust. God is entrusting you with his Word; trusting you to handle it properly and to follow the Holy Spirit in taking it to where and how it's needed. To do that you must keep your head on straight.

EGO: Everyone's Got One

There can be no substantive discussion about keeping your head on straight without giving attention to the understanding of the role of the ego. The ego is somewhat misunderstood so it gets a bad rap. The definition of the ego changed from the original Freudian thought to the common understanding that it's the measure of what a person thinks of him/herself. A person who thinks highly of their self is said to have a "big ego;" this thing inside that gets out of control, grows into a big monster that causes everyone to hate you. Wrong! It isn't about size, big ego, little ego, no ego. It's about a healthy vs. an unhealthy ego. Don't skip this section.

Per the psychoanalytic theory of Sigmund Freud, there are three parts to the personality, the Id, Superego, and Ego defined as follows:

- **Id**: The instinctual, biological part of self. The id wants what it wants; whatever feels good at the time; no consideration for reality or consequences. Its sole motivation is instant gratification or the "pleasure principle[f]."

- **Superego**: The social part of your personality; your conscience.

- **The Ego**: The conscious decision making component. The ego prevents us from acting irrationally on the desires created by the id. It tries to balance the idealistic standards of the Superego and has the complex task of dealing with the realities of the external world.

The id, superego, and ego work together in creating a behavior. The id creates the demands; the ego adds the needs of reality with the superego adding morality to the action which is taken. Our behavior is determined by the interaction of these three components.

---

[f] The Pleasure Principle is the desire for immediate gratification vs. the deferral of gratification. It drives one to seek pleasure and to avoid pain

For this discussion, the ego will be the focus of attention because the ego is the component responsible for keeping your head on straight. The ego interacts with the other components in this way: It's like software that tells the other components how to work, allowing you to interact with the world in a proper and acceptable manner. Freud made the analogy of the id being a horse while the ego is the rider. The ego is 'like a man on horseback, who has to hold in check the superior strength of the horse.' (Freud, 1923, p.15). If the ego is healthy, the rest of the personality will stay balanced.

The Healthy Ego (THE: The Healthy Ego)

The healthy ego is controlled by the "Reality Principle.[8]" The reality principle causes the ego to consider the pros and cons of a desire before deciding to act on it. The ego doesn't try to stop these desires, but tries to achieve them in realistic and acceptable ways. A healthy ego is an ego under control. When you have an urge to do something that you know is inappropriate, the healthy ego (THE) is what prevents you from acting on these urges.

When you make decisions, set personal boundaries, and maintain self-esteem, take care of yourself, feel good about who you are, and you stand by your values, these are signs of a healthy ego. If the ego is functioning as designed, it operates beneath the radar. That, however, doesn't happen naturally. Will power alone isn't strong enough to keep the ego in a healthy state. It takes divine health care from heaven and the cost of premiums is prayer. It's when the ego becomes unhealthy that it steps onto center stage.

---

[8] The Reality Principle leads us to delay gratification and behave in ways that satisfies the id's desires in realistic and socially appropriate ways. It weighs the costs and benefits of an action before deciding to act upon or abandon an impulse.

The Unhealthy Ego (**EGW**: Ego Gone Wild)

An Ego Gone Wild (EGW) is the Ego in an unhealthy state. EGW is a "virus" that attacks the ego, the condition which is easily identifiable in others but virtually unrecognizable in one's self. It's when your ego's software gets a virus that the dramas begin. EGW virus makes you look like a fool and you're unaware of it.[h]

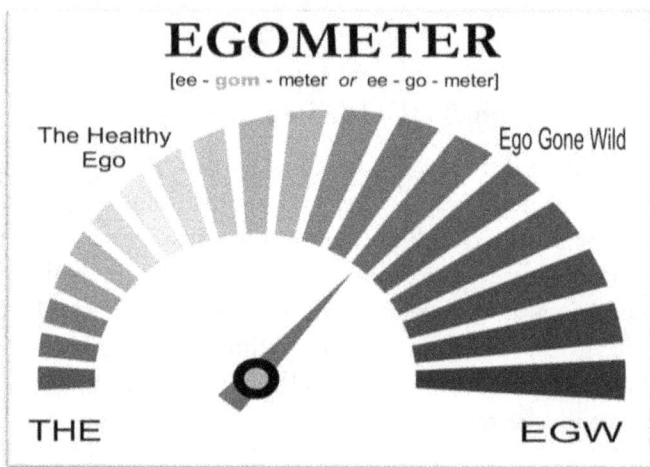

EGOMETER
[ee - gom - meter *or* ee - go - meter]

The Healthy Ego

Ego Gone Wild

THE

EGW

Seven Symptoms of The EGW Virus

1. All roads lead to you

You love the sound of your own voice. You don't look at the person with whom you're supposedly in conversation. When they're talking, you're not listening to them. You're planning what you're going to say next. No matter what the conversation, somehow the focus always turns back to you.

[h] See EGW Quick Check-up & Treatment at the end of this chapter

2. Whosoever has an ear must hear

Not everyone needs or wants to hear your story, what you're doing or planning to do. Ask yourself: Did anyone ask me for details? Is it necessary that I share this? What am I getting out of this? Why am I so insistent?" Stop! Check the needle on your Egometer.[i]

3. You've got to be right all the time

It's okay to back down sometimes, really. That doesn't mean you've changed your opinion or admitting you're wrong. It just means you're giving up trying to shove it into someone else's brain. You can't control what other people think. They may be wrong but so what! On the other hand, you may be wrong. If you feel your boundaries or principles are being violated, speak up. But if it's the EGW virus, back off and be the bigger person.

4. You think you're doing it all yourself

You're never doing it all. Your EGW will make you think that you're the only one pulling the wagon. The truth is, there's a support team around you, visible or invisible. No matter how insignificant you think their contribution, they're part of the team that got you where you are. Acknowledge others. If you think no one did anything for you, check the needle on your Egometer.

5. Being defensive

What are you defending anyway? Your terrified, fragile ego? What would happen if you considered another view? It wouldn't kill you and it might make you smarter. Give it a shot. You'd be surprised how often giving honest consideration when you normally give knee jerk opposition to things that used to upset you now seem interesting or

---

[i] Egometer (Ego-meter): Fictional metaphor: A mental meter that measures the "in the moment" health of your ego

helpful. Withholding a reaction doesn't mean you're agreeing, it just means you're secure enough in yourself to give things a second thought.

6. Interrupting / Not Listening

You don't always have to say what you think. Listen, observe, learn. Listening is powerful. It cultivates allegiance. It affirms others. People will love you if you listen to them. What do you have better to do? God has brought each person into your life for a reason. If you listen long enough, you'll discover their purpose in your life. Remember: those who say, don't know. And those who know, don't say.

7. Always able to Justify Yourself

It's difficult to watch someone dig themselves deeper into a hole with weak rationale when they could simply acknowledge the wrong and be done with it.

To keep your head on straight for some is a monumental challenge, for others it's merely a test from time to time. You'll need to internalize some things before you get started so they'll be in your sphere of reference throughout your career. Preaching is the most visible of all the public ministries. In addition to the Sunday pulpit there's television ministries, terrestrial and internet radio, live streaming, social networks, and countless other cyberspace avenues that contribute to the exaltation of the call and/or the person in the call. People will lovingly and without malice put the preacher on a pedestal. Cultural tradition and lack of theological knowledge of the spiritual gifts make it easy to ascribe to the preacher "celebrity" status. In many cases the elevated perception of the preacher is rooted in ethnic/generational thought. It's the call or the office that's exalted and not the person in the call. The accolades the preacher may enjoy are byproducts of the reverence for the office regardless of who's sitting in the seat. That's simply the norm in some faith traditions. Keeping that in mind will help you stay grounded.

There are some who aren't answering "the call" but rather pursuing the position because they desire the recognition and favor that comes with it. Is that you? Be honest because if it is, you'll be struggling with it for the duration of the time you stand in the call that isn't yours. You may as well start with your head on straight. When the favor of the people seems to follow you around, your ego can only operate in a healthy way if you're in the right place. Rather than trying to change the dynamics, your time and energy will be far better spent keeping yourself grounded and doing what you've been called to do regardless of public perception. To that end, three concepts come to mind, Sobriety, Humility, and Readiness.

On Sobriety

The word sobriety initially suggests the state of being free and in control of one's self, no longer under the self-destructive influence of external stimuli; specifically, drug or alcohol free. Free of addiction, no longer dependent upon or hooked on any psychoactive drug, psychopharmaceutic, or psychotropic chemical substance that changes brain function resulting in alterations in perception, mood, or consciousness. Under the influence of a chemical substance, regardless of its legality, the effects are the same; blurred vision, impaired judgment, your sense of reason skewed. You can't be trusted and you can't trust yourself.

You can also be under the influence of the wrong person(s), involved in unhealthy relationships, entangled in unfavorable associations, even ideologies that impair your mental health in the same way as substance abuse. Under the influence, to a greater or lesser degree, is a state of not being fully in control of what you think, your sense of reasoning, or choices you make, vulnerable to the strength of the external influence.

Paul broadens the scope of the conversation even further as he warns of another influence that threatens to compromise mental sobriety. You. He says, think with a sober mind; use sober judgment and don't think more of yourself than you ought to think. Imagine that! Paul links sobriety with having a balanced perception of yourself when he says not to think more highly of yourself than you ought to think. Ought is the word that sticks out. Clearly there is the suggestion to think positively of yourself, but the word "ought" suggests there's a boundary or line between positive self-thought and being unbalanced under the influence of conceit. You can love yourself so much that you get high on yourself, believe your own press, get swept away in the cries of the crowd, "Hosanna, Hosanna," becoming unable to receive wise counsel. Don't underestimate the detriment that can be.

Get a grip on yourself!

A very well known, highly respected prelate said in a televised sermon, "You don't correct me. I'm not to be corrected. We can talk about it but you don't correct me. I'm not a child." That's dangerously close, if not over the borderline of "ought." Who is anyone to say they are not to be corrected? Everyone needs correction from time to time. Not a child? There is childlikeness within everyone, perhaps more than is recognized, that pushes or sets in motion less than perfect choices. You don't get to decide from where or from whom your correction comes. Keep check on your ego-meter. It's God's prerogative to orchestrate correction. It's our "ought" to accept it. It's certainly important to acknowledge and appreciate your gifts from the Holy Spirit, but equally important is balance and the proper perspective.

'Tis true, God has a plan for your life and it's good, but the world has not been awaiting your arrival. Peter says "Gird up the loins of your mind ..." In other words, get a grip on yourself. You're a vessel God created and gifted the vessel for his purpose. Preaching isn't about who you are, it's about who God is. It's what you do and how you carry yourself as you live and walk in the life to which you are called. The responsibilities inherent in the call are many but one of the most important is that you're always aware of your ambassadorship. You represent someone greater than yourself, and a purpose grander than your own. You're an integral part of a strategic plan that began in eternity past, transcends the now, and extends to eternity future. People are looking at you, and looking up to you; and when they look, they need to see a well-balanced, *ego under Holy Ghost control* person. They need to see someone who knows Jesus more than just on a first name basis.

One of the most difficult things in the walk of this call is to live the sermons you've preached, and personally answer the questions you've asked of others. Although referred to as such for conceptual reasons, the sermon is more than an event or a moment; and surely not a performance. It's a divine communication for both the preacher and the hearers. The difference is you, the preacher, must hear the message, prepare the message, receive it unto yourself, then deliver it. While preparing, and pouring into others, in addition to keeping pace with the demands of your own life, it's easy to unintentionally skip the step: receiving the message unto yourself. But, if you should ever stumble into the moment when you hear the echoes of your voice, that, beloved, is sobering.

On Humility

Humility is one of those almost nebulous concepts that despite what a dictionary says, it's difficult to precisely define and certainly challenging to describe. It isn't something you can see, although some interpret physical expressions and appearances as humility. Some synonyms are modesty and meekness; each of which may manifest itself in different ways in differing scenarios. Humility isn't tangible or visual. It's something experienced from another person as you interrelate. It's something you see in a person as they interact with the world and situations around them. It's genuine and real; doesn't come and go nor can it be turned on and off. Humility is a state of mental being informed

13

by one's perception of themselves in juxtaposition to their perception of God; a perception of self in relationship with God revealed situationally. In other words, it would be impossible for a person having a realistic understanding of the awesomeness of God in relationship to themselves, to have an inflated view of themselves, or an EGW.[j]

Humility behaves with a quiet, powerful strength. It calms the annoyance of deadlines because it understands time in eternity; God's time. It isn't driven by competition because it rests in the fact that "what God has for me is for me." Humility trumps jealousy because it understands the concept of running your own race. It prevails against the temptation to envy another's success because it understands how to be grateful for the blessings of others. Humility stills the frustration of delayed satisfaction because it understands the rewards for waiting.

Some are born with a personality that lends itself to a more humble spirit than perhaps others. In others, it may have been developed early in life through teaching. Yet others, for whom humility isn't second nature, it takes a little work. In fairness to those for whom humility is a struggle, consider this. On a whole, the culture of the western world, a capitalistic society, places little value on anything that can't be parlayed into the bottom line, consequently humility isn't necessarily seen as a useful character trait. So, give yourself a bit of a break as you struggle to develop a strength in your character that gets little endorsement or affirmation in the social milieu to which you're accustomed. Self-assess your level of humility. Slow down, pause now and then. Ease your foot up from the gas pedal of your determination, ambitions, and motivations; shift into park on a regular basis. Put "the Will of God" in your divine navigation system. Discern the mind of God on your forward movement.

---

[j] EGW Ego Gone Wild. See "Ego Gone Wild," pg. 8

Humility is looking Godward with self-surrender and sincere desire for God's Will not only in what you're doing but in how you navigate in and through relationships. James and Peter both agree that God gives grace to the humble[k]. We have only a notion of the incomprehensible value of Grace so if God gives his Grace for humility, then he must place a high premium on humility. It's completely natural as well as a fundamental value in our competitive society to want to do better, and aspire to be the best. It's incredibly important that you understand this point. There's a fine line between the kingdom of this world and the kingdom of God. As a preacher, you're called to understand both worlds and keep your eye on the fine line. Of course, you don't want to rest even for a moment in mediocrity, however, your better and your best aren't defined by comparison, therefore competition holds no true value in the God's sphere. God defines success. God defines greatness. Humility advises, "You're not better than anyone else. You're not worse than anyone else. Just be your-self. Be your best self.

On Readiness

The meal is ready to eat when the food on the table. The cake is ready when the oven timer sounds. The baby is ready to be born when the contractions begin. Every call, every new ministry, every God breathed idea has a gestation period, a learning curve, a process to readiness. It takes time and some things just can't be rushed. The wisdom is to know when you're ready.

When you're called to preach you're not ready to preach. The call is for you to get ready to preach and all that comes with it. The desire may be strong and the gifts of a skilled orator evident to everyone around you, but when the call comes, you're not ready. You're called to get ready. As with most things, you

---

[k] I Peter 5:5; James 4:6

15

can't see much beyond the now. The realities unfold as you travel your journey. You're called to prepare for the life of a preacher, to cultivate the mind of a preacher, and to develop the strength and wisdom for the tasks of a preacher. You may have been in church all your life, well acquainted with the Word of God, and have lots of preacher friends in your network; though there are common sites in the landscape, the journey of every preaching ministry is different. Your ministry of preaching will not be the same as any you've seen. God doesn't need replicas. He's looking for authenticity. He wants those who are able to embrace who he has made them to be and willing to cultivate their voice to be heard by the ones who need to hear the message he has for them. There're a few things you need to know before you go. One of the things Paul speaks of is gifts and how they differ according to the grace and proportion of faith given to us.[1] It's personal so that we can't do it like someone else. He makes a point about waiting. As exciting as the preaching ministry may look, - wait.

David was anointed to be king of Israel but he had to wait about 15 years from the time he was first anointed by Samuel to the time he became king over Judah. It was another seven years before David was anointed king over all of Israel. That means David waited over 20 years of his life before becoming king over all of Israel. David didn't quit his job as a shepherd and run to the royal apparel store to buy his robe and crown. He remained faithful in his position as shepherd and serving as King Saul's armor bearer and private musician; serving the king he would ultimately replace. This isn't to suggest you'll be waiting over 20 years for your preaching ministry to begin. It is to say that even after you are sure of your call to preach you may serve in different capacities before you ever step up to the mic behind the sacred desk.

----

[1] Romans 12:6-7a

You may be asked to teach bible study at a nursing home where the participants are at different levels of dementia; or perhaps in their right mind and you're their only connection to church which may have been a vital part of their lives before being confined to the nursing home. You may receive invitations to preach in a storefront church or a house church identified with the name in magic marker on a piece of cardboard, with barely 15 people present including children. You may preach and your offering is less than $25.00. These are opportunities; opportunities to preach like you're preaching to thousands. Opportunities to feel a connection with the pew; to learn to meet people where they are; to speak the language of the people. It's your time of "becoming." Beginnings may be less than what you imagined but don't be discouraged. Before birth there is gestation. Your birthday is coming.

Waiting is uncomfortable, no matter what you're waiting for. While waiting, you may see others called after you go out before you and in your opinion, less gifted and less ready. Just remember, the Holy Spirit is preparing you and grooming you for your ministry, not theirs. Don't compare your track with anyone else's. You can't run their race; neither should you try. As uncomfortable and frustrating as the preparation time may feel, don't skip it, shortcut or circumvent it. Your readiness is essential and specific to you. Being patient with your divinely customized process of preparation will yield great reward over the lifetime of your ministry.

You don't have to accept every invitation to preach that comes your way. In fact, you shouldn't accept every invitation that's extended. That's difficult to wrap your mind around if you're just starting out. You know God has called you to preach. You've gotten past the doubt and struggle in discerning the voice of God on the matter of your call. You're willing to do God's Will, go where he wants you to go, a zeal in your spirit and

On Your Mark!

Get Set!!

WAIT!!!

obedience in your heart. READY! SET!! NO!!! Wait a minute!!!!

The call has come, why wait? Word of Wisdom: Well-meaning individuals will invite you to be the "preacher of the hour" wanting to help you along, give you an opportunity to preach. Feels nice, right? Wait! Because they recommended your name doesn't mean the Holy Spirit submitted your name. Not every opportunity is your opportunity. "Fools rush in where angels fear to tread.[m]" Be careful not to allow yourself to be pushed to the mic before you're ready, or stand to preach before a congregation wherein you're outclassed. It feels good to be invited to preach but not so good if the engagement turns out to be ill timed for your readiness. If you're not ready for the engagement, you could embarrass yourself, your pastor, your spouse, family, and the person who extended the invitation. It's okay to say "No, thank you." You need a mentor and you must learn to discern. Sit with yourself and ponder some thoughts and answer a few questions.

I'll never forget an experience very early in my call. A wonderful woman who owned a catering facility gave an annual event for pastors. She didn't know me but wanted to be supportive of this young female preacher so she asked me to be the guest preacher. I felt neither excitement or nervousness. True to my task oriented nature, I accepted the engagement as a responsibility, nothing more. I didn't even ask if there was an honorarium. My pastor, at the time, wasn't supportive of women in ministry so he didn't mentor me as he did my male counterparts. Whatever advice I was able to glean came while sitting quietly, not included at the main table, or while serving the male preachers their food at meetings; essentially from whatever I was able to overhear from their conversations. That's just how it was in those days.

---

[m] Alexander Pope's An essay on criticism, 1709

I thought if my pastor heard I'd done a good job he'd be proud of me and take me under his wing like the rest of the associates. If not, surely with all the "big dogs" in the room, someone will want to mentor this young woman of God. So, well prepared sermon notes in hand, big beautiful bible with gold edged pages, and fully clothed in spiritual naivety, I stepped up to the mic that night. With polished pulpit manners, and corporate professionalism, I honored the proper protocol and began the sermon. Less than five minutes into the message a cloud seemed to lift from my eyes. Looking back at me in a sea of dark suits, white shirts, and non-distinctive ties were cold eyes glaring from the grave, unexpressive faces of the quintessential "princes of the pulpit" of the day. I knew I was dead in the water. I thought, "God, the only way you can help me is to open up a hole in the floor and let me fall in it." I continued, not hearing the sound of my own voice as I struggled to find a way to end the nightmare. When I got in my car, I rested my head on the steering wheel, with tears in my eyes and said, God, I'll do this but you have to send someone. I have no one who's "been there, done that," and who cares about me in ministry. I don't know what I don't know. He sent Prathia Hall, who, for eleven years before she went home to be with the Lord, unselfishly poured into me with her time, guidance, wisdom, encouragement, more than I could ever have asked or imagined.

If you have a pastor who will mentor and teach you, who'll filter your invitations to preach before you accept them, be ever grateful, for that's a wonderful gift not to be taken for granted. If not, ask God to send someone upon whose heart your name is written and in whose eyes is God's vision for you; who'll care about your level of readiness, gifts, skills, and whether your maturity in ministry is equal to the level of the engagement. You need to be under authority, under someone who can see the landscape at a level of which you cannot.

Dispel the guilt in saying "No." God always has a remnant so if you say "No" until you're ready, someone else will preach and that's okay. The mistake many preachers make is the failure to handle their call with wisdom, prudence and abundance of caution. Some Christians bristle at the idea of referring to anything related to the church as business. Hear this again. Get a grip on yourself! Your call and everything associated with it is your responsibility. It's more than the sermon. You must handle your ministry and the business of your ministry that God has entrusted into your care or it will be raggedy. It's your responsibility to protect its image and reputation. No one likes a raggedy preacher – and that has nothing to do with clothing.

So, the question is, "How does one gain the experience needed if they say 'No' to invitations. Join or create an accountability group, more commonly called a ministerial group. Meet regularly. Once a week is advisable, for at least two hours. Talk, share, take turns preaching and be strong enough to accept criticism. Be sure there are a couple of seasoned preachers in the group, not just neophytes, the blind leading the blind. Seasoned preachers will welcome the opportunity to help groom you for the ministry. Be deliberate about honing your craft. If you're not in seminary, find a good bible institute to attend. Online is great but when it comes to preaching you need to be in the presence of others. Remember, the more professionally you handle yourself, the more confidence people will have in you.

	Head Check	Yes ✓	No ✓
1.	**On Sobriety** God called me because I'm awesome, gifted and ready.		
2.	**On Humility** I understand, appreciate, and honor the gifts of others, and how I need them to be my best.		
3.	**On Readiness** I'm in ongoing training: seminars, webinars, seminary, online courses?		
4.	I write sermons even when I don't have a preaching engagement.		
5.	I would accept the engagement if I knew the honorarium would be only $25.00?		
6.	I can name at least three preachers, whom I know personally, whose preaching gift I admire, and I can explain why?		
7.	I can decline an invitation to preach, without annoyance, if my pastor feels I'm not ready for it?		
8.	I could decline an invitation to preach if I feel the timing isn't right for me?		

EGW Virus Quick Check-Up
Seven Symptoms & Treatment

	Symptoms	Y	N	Treatment
1	All roads lead to me			Consider the heavens, the work of God's fingers the moon and the stars,[n]
2	Whosoever has an ear must hear me			But in humility consider others more important than yourselves.[o]
3	I must be right all the time			A wise person will hear and increase in learning, a person of understanding will acquire wise counsel[p]
4	I think I'm doing it all w/o help			There's a hidden army of help around you. Open your eyes.[q]
5	I'm defensive			
6	I interrupt others. I don't listen.			A fool takes no pleasure in understanding, but only in expressing his opinion[r]
7	I justify myself even when it makes no sense			Give instruction to a wise man and he will be still wiser, teach a righteous man and he will increase his learning.[s]

---

[n] Psalm 8:3, 4
[o] Philippians 2:3b
[p] Proverbs 1:5
[q] 2 Kings 6:17
[r] Proverbs 18:2
[s] Proverbs 9:9

PRAYERFULLY PONDER

1. What does it mean to be down-to-earth about self-perception and how you see others?

_____

_____

_____

_____

2. What does it mean to be realistic about your vision for yourself and how to get there?

_____

_____

_____

_____

3. What are the priorities in your life now and how do they fit in or relate to preaching?

_____

_____

_____

_____

Rabbi Zusya (1718–1800), an Orthodox rabbi and an early Hasidic luminary was renowned throughout the world for his insights as a scholar, teacher, and healer. When he was an old man he grew nervous as he thought about the world to come, his life and how little he had done. He began to imagine what the angel who would meet him might ask.

"Why were you not a Moses?" He thought, I shall answer with conviction, 'Because I was not born to be a Moses.' "And if the angel challenges me, 'But neither did you perform the feats of Elijah.' Again, he thought, I shall firmly respond, 'My mission was not the same as that of Elijah.'" But there is one question he feared God would ask and he'd be unable to answer: 'Why were you not a Rabbi Zusya?

THE 2ND COMMANDMENT

THOU SHALL BE THINE AUTHENTIC SELF

THINK FOR A MOMENT. ARE YOU BEING your real self? Do you know? The question has nothing to do with wigs, toupees, cosmetic enhancements, or anything related to outward appearance. Those things are your choices, adornments that change with styles and fashion. Your authentic self is what lives vibrantly through or lies silently beneath what's visible. Authenticity means genuine; real; not false or copied. What was first, at the root, the core? What was there before anything else ever was? Authenticity, then, begins with who God created you to be; who you are on the inside. Your authentic self is the genuine you, not a copy of someone else, who you look like or what you do for a living. Your authentic self is your unique you, who you are, your passions, values, what you think, how you think, how you process and interact with the world, your personality, temperament, and disposition. Your authenticity begins with God.

Are you a patient person? A tolerant person? A compassionate person? Are you free spirited, comfortable with ambiguity, or do you prefer structure? Are you an "inside the box" or an "outside the box" person? Are you laid back or assertive? Are you a nine to five person or do you work until the job is done? Do you naturally take the lead in situations even without the title? The questions can go on and on. There is no subliminal judgment in any of the questions, no good or bad, right, or wrong. Everyone is different; everyone is valid in their personality, style; their created being. Every person is a creative expression of God's image, each reflecting parts of the infinite facets of God's self.

There are several instruments that define personality types, work styles, leadership styles, etc. While you don't want to get bogged down or obsessed with the instruments, they're helpful in a couple of ways. While not culturally objective, they present an outline of the personality and leadership styles, giving you a larger view of the array of types and where you may theoretically find your definition. Consistent with your level of open-mindedness, engaging in the instruments can be intimidating or informative. Have fun with them. They're not meant to be conclusive, only thought provoking. Approach them broadmindedly, without preconceived notions and that will decrease the element of judgment and bias normally brought to an experience. View the results as a guide or a window through which to gain insight into yourself. No one, except God, knows you better than you do. Personality and work style instrument often help you to get to know yourself a little better.

Secondly, it's important to have a general understanding of your personality type. It goes a long way in learning to accept and appreciate yourself, the person God created. It also helps in the understanding of the unique ways in which the Holy Spirit guides and uses you in the Kingdom of God.

Being your authentic self is living from the inside out, interacting with the world through the lens and grid of who you really are. Who you are on the inside has nothing to do with what others are thinking or saying about you. Your authentic self is the "you" who never changes. You may hide your you, disguise your you, or even try to kill your you by trying to be someone else, but your authentic self will always be there waiting for affirmation and opportunities for expression. There is a need for the real you in the world or God would not have bothered to create you if you weren't somehow necessary in his overall eternal plan. You have a voice that only certain one's can hear. You have a style that only certain ones can relate to. You have "a way" that only certain ones will follow. Paul says, God will supply all of our needs. You are the need of someone or something in God's plan. Start wrapping your mind around that thought. No, you're not the "itness of the allness," or the "end all to be all," but recognizing the intentionality of your being is the perfect place to begin. God, our creator, uniquely designed every person. He wasn't having a bad day when he came up with your blueprint. You're not a mistake, an "OOPS!" or afterthought, substitute, or an addendum, but part of the divine tapestry of time, the bigger picture, set in motion before the foundation of the world. You have a specific purpose, a strategic part, a role to play in the drama of eternity, but to see the beauty of it all you must come unpretentiously to the life experience. It's a choice.

> To come to the life experience unpretentiously is a choice

Consider for a moment, Spiritual Gifts. Paul takes time to talk about spiritual gifts and the precision of their operation. Insight reveals that while different personality types operate in each of the gifts, there are certain personality types more suited for certain gifts. Being your authentic self, the self who God created in you positions you to function with excellence in your respective spiritual gift(s) and calling.

There is a cultural habit of comparing one's self to others; against biased standards of beauty; socially defined definitions of success and accomplishment; against others who've reached a level of celebrity or notoriety to which one may admire or aspire. At an early age, well-meaning voices dictate what to think of yourself, what the world thinks of you, what to think of the world around you and how to fit into it, … or not.

Nurturing, social grooming, mentoring is good and necessary, and you're blessed when it comes from those who love and desire to see you grow into your best self. Be aware, however, there are other voices eager to be heard, shaping your perceptions with the fruit of their life experience of narrow vision, dwarfed goals, and sight walking. Rhetoric that constructs walls around you, giving you a box to live in, fostering a world view limited to their own.

Sound bites, highway billboards, overt and covert messages coming at you every minute of the day telling you how you ought to look, how you should think and feel, what you should buy, and what/who you ought to be. Carefully crafted marketing strategies using subliminal suggestions that feed your demons of destructive self-images, self-hatred, self-doubt and low self-esteem plant the seeds of inadequacy watered with doubt, artfully conspiring to convince you, first, that there is a problem, and, secondly, that the problem is "You." You're not good enough. You need to be a better you, a more appealing you, a more successful you. You're too much of this or not enough of that, but there's a solution just for you that will bring you to that subjective standard of "perfection." The message is clear:

Many spend a lifetime trying to find someone else to be

You aren't good enough as you are. You need to be fixed. Truth is not the measure and reality is not the issue. Keeping you focused outwardly is the means to prevent you from seeing inwardly, blinding you to your inner treasure and the beauty of your authentic self.

Many spend their lifetime trying to find someone else to be, copying this one and mimicking that one, thinking someone else is somehow better. So deeply rooted that it becomes second nature to look outwardly for the solution to becoming "the better you." So much a part of your sub consciousness that you pass it down to your children. So engrained in your psyche that you judge yourself and others by the perceptions continuously cultivated in your minds over your lifetime.

It's no wonder precious people of God lose their sense of themselves long before ever having an opportunity to become aware of their true selves and appreciate who they are as a wonderful, planned creation of God with a divine purpose and an intentional future. You are anointed to be you. You're your own worst critic, finding what you perceive as flaws in yourself, even sometimes asking God why he made you this way. BUT! to whom are you comparing yourself? Against whose standard are you measuring yourself? Certainly, you should smooth edges and rid yourself of destructive behaviors and habits that masquerade as second nature. You should stir up and perfect your gifts and talents, but surely not change who you are. You're not approved because you're perfect, you're approved because of to whom you belong. To be your authentic self you have to know your you, and accept yourself as a good product of God's work that day; the reality of his imagination, perfect imperfections, flaws and all. Whatever you are, too much of this and not enough of that, you are perfectly shaped and fashioned to do what you were created to do.

You are anointed to be you

The desire to matter, fit in, be accepted, have recognition, a sense of purpose and belonging can be very strong, leading you to become unduly influenced, giving up your capacity of pure, free, independent thought to the degree necessary to feel accepted and affirmed. Using a grassroots term, that's "selling yourself cheap." When you relinquish your power of self-validation to others, adapting yourself to what you think you should be without giving yourself the benefit of seeking to know and cultivate the person God has created you to be; without a positive, healthy

Identity Theft

29

and confident self-awareness, you will seek to be someone else; a copycat; a fraud. No! No! No! That's *Identity Theft.* A borrowed identity just won't do. To find value in being someone else is an insult to your authentic self, as well as the God who made you.

You may be inspired by others and try to develop similar qualities of character, but those qualities will be expressed through your own person. When you're content with yourself, comfortable in your own skin, you don't compare or compete with others. You can look with admiration at others, their accomplishments, and elevations, hear the accolades and applause, and be genuinely happy for them without feeling slighted or passed over. It's in the knowing that "what God has for you is for you. It's in knowing your spiritual gifts and calling, passion and purpose that allows you to rise above the low state of envy and jealousy because you know who you are in Christ. When you're not trying to be something or someone you're not, there's an incredible peace that abides on the inside, and rest from having to be "on" all the time.

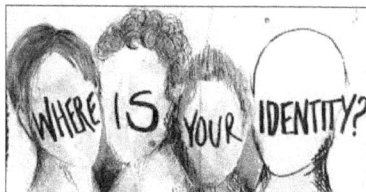

What is Your Authentic Self?

> "I am nobody but myself."
> -- Ralph Ellison

When you set yourself free to be yourself, you never have to think about how to be yourself. You just do what comes naturally. Do you! "Free to be me" isn't that self-indulgent philosophy of hedonism. It's a mental posture that allows the freedom to grow into what God would have you to be, and finding joy in being that.

Children get it, but somewhere along the way, lose it. Listen to this funny but insightful wisdom in an exchange between three children as one was teasing and mimicking the other:

Lex: Don't copy me!

Nip: But you're so cute.

Lex: I know, but you don't get to be cute by being a copycat.

Nip: OK, then how did you get so cute?

Lex: God made me that way. That's how.

Nip: How can I get cute like you?

Lex: You can't get cute like me, Boo. You have to get cute like you. That's the way God works.

Dove: That's right, and God made me cuter than all y'all!

Your authentic self is your "cute." It's your "you;" your unique you. You know when you've found your cute when you can say, I'm okay with me. I'm comfortable with me. I like me.

Authenticity is an easy concept to entertain when talking about artwork or antiques; but not so easy in the context of self and on the very personal level of self-examination. What does the real you look like? What makes you uniquely you? Even the thought of engaging in self-exploration to answer those questions can be quite intimidating. You don't know what or who you might find. Suppose "I don't like what I find?" Ok, that's an understandable fear. Remember, everything starts with God. In Genesis chapter one, in the beginning of all creation, as God completed the various entities it tells us that he saw that "it was good." Say it with me, "I'm the manifestation of God's creative imagination." When he finished creating you, he saw that you were good. He likes what he did. He loves you. The Holy Spirit will guide you to a new and true vision of yourself as you make finding, accepting and being your authentic self an intentional part of your spiritual development.

31

What does authenticity have to do with preaching?

It has much to do with preaching. The preacher is the bearer of the message. The sermon begins before the preacher opens his or her mouth. You speak before you say a word. Authenticity speaks with a loud voice. It attracts others. People are drawn to those who are comfortable in their own skin. Others feel comfortable and secure in your self-confidence. If you're masquerading as someone else, perhaps a preacher you admire or one whose success you desire, then you're always acting, never being.

> How can you preach about a creative God if you can't live in the uniqueness he created in you?

The absence of authenticity brings the sermon into question. Is the sermon you're preaching one that drawn breath in your spirit first? Are you re-preaching a sermon that "worked" for another preacher. If the sermon begins before you say a word, then everything about you is an introduction to the sermon and part of the sermon. Your style. Is it you? Or are you copying someone else? Your speech. Is it you? Or are you mimicking someone else? Your delivery. Is it you? Or are you channeling someone else? How can you preach about a creative God without living out the uniqueness within yourself.? God never meant for you to be the same as any other preacher or he could have created clones. God created all things, distinction in all things and beauty in the distinction. What is your distinction? What makes you distinctively, authentically you?

Your personality, your approach to life in general, what you bring to the scripture largely determines what you look for in the scriptures and what you bring out of it. Some things you just can't fake no matter how hard you try. You may imitate preaching style, physical expressions, voice inflections, even little idioms from another preacher but imitation becomes transparent when it comes to the message. You can't preach with authenticity what you don't believe, what you don't embrace within yourself. You may give sound to the words but you can't fake authenticity and without authenticity there is no power. You may turn up the volume but there will be no power. In other words, a negative, grumpy person can't preach about joy with any degree of spiritual integrity. No one would believe them. A judgmental person will have difficulty preaching about the blessedness of God's outpouring of grace and favor, and the free gift of salvation because a judgmental preacher wants you to pay for your sins and wear your sorrow.

If you're an old fogy, fuddy duddy, who holds onto the way things used to be (and you can be that at 35 years old), you can't preach about the new things waiting in an exciting new future. You can't preach Isaiah 42:9 or 43:19. How can you embrace the tools of technology, and social media if you're holding fast to the past? You can't preach what you can't embrace. You can't preach what you don't have in you because the thinly veiled façade soon breaks down. Authenticity has everything to do with preaching.

Finding Your Own Voice

Your voice begins with God. Voice in this context isn't the audible sound that comes out of your mouth when you preach; it isn't volume or decibels. Your voice is your interpretations; the result of that which flows through your unique grid system on its way to becoming speech. Your voice begins with you in the Potter's hand; God molding and distinctively creating not just the vessel but the way the vessel receives, digests thoughts and feels. You're recognizable by what you say and how you say it. Your voice is distinctive. It's your signature. It's the sound of your personality, your personalized way of interpreting things and presenting them. Your voice reflects your passions, gifts, that about which you care deeply, the totality of your life experiences; your testimonies, and the wisdom you've gained from your joys and sorrows; so much so that the Holy Spirit can use any or all of it to empower the Word

33

you preach.   Your voice is what makes your message particular and alive.   Someone can take five of your sermons, and given you haven't stolen them from another preacher,[t] they can get a sense of who you are.

Read this paragraph carefully with an open mind.   The Bible says in both accounts of the Gospel, Matthew and Luke that what comes out of our mouths is that which is in our heart. This is, in part, why different preachers can preach from the identical text and the sermon come across differently. Without knowing it, the preacher relates to or finds something of himself or herself in the text.   Subconsciously or not, regardless of the amount of study the preacher runs the text through their personal grid system and what comes out has a little or a lot of themselves woven into the sermon.   Back in the old days there were preachers known as "sin preachers."   They could find sin in the way you brushed your teeth, highly judgmental, very limited on grace.   They could make forgiveness so conditional that it sounded more like a threat.   You knew them.   You didn't have to go to the revival to know what they were going to preach. You knew their voice.   There were no "grace notes" in the melody of their messages.   Conversely, another preacher could preach about sin and make you happy to repent because of the way they presented grace.   That's voice.

The buzz word is "brand."   Your voice is your brand.   Is your voice familiar even to you?   How would you describe your brand?   If your life could speak, what would it say?   What are you known for as a preacher in the kingdom realm?   If you were an instrument, which one would it be and how would you sound? Poignant questions yet many preachers exhaust themselves hiding in someone else's brand, never asking the questions.   Be bold.   Ask the questions, then take the time to answer yourself.

---

[t] The 8th Commandment, Thou Shall Not Steal

What do I think about this or that? My opinions, the things I espouse and express; are they what I believe or what's been passed down to me or I've heard from others? Is it what my mind, my spirit, and my emotions have discussed with the scriptures? Do I know my own mind? Does this really sound like me? That will be revisited a little later in this section.

Finding your voice means discovering your comfort zone, the courage to give full expression in your sermons through your true self. It's about the story you tell (message) and how you tell it (voice). When you think of your voice, think of your purpose. Is it to motivate, inspire, teach, challenge, comfort encourage, empower, ...? Your purpose will come through in your messages. The Biblical stories have been told thousands of times, through thousands of messages and messengers over thousands of years. In preaching, your message isn't just words on a manuscript, it's God's message communicated through your voice. No one can say it the way you say it. No one can feel the meaning and express it the way you can.

Developing your authentic voice takes time, courage, and practice. It means overcoming the fear of being yourself and letting go of what others think is "preaching." Sometimes you don't yet know what your true voice sounds like because you've been mimicking others for so long; preaching it like Bishop Rev. Dr. Wonderful. It takes self-excavation, daring to discover what you have buried deep within, or what has been buried by any number of influences around you: culture, church, workplace, family. When you can understand that you have a voice that is exclusively yours to develop and to share, you'll stop allowing yourself to be diminished by mimicking the voice of others. You'll no longer define yourself in comparison to another preacher or based on what others are doing or saying. The next time you feel yourself starting to compare yourself to others, **STOP!** Remind yourself that you have your own voice, unique to you, to your message, and to your calling.

On the day of Pentecost, the Holy Spirit made quite a dramatic entrance into the upper room. The sound of a mighty rushing wind, tongues of fire. WOW! A diverse multitude of people heard the Gospel in the language of their own nationality or ethnicity. There was only one preacher and the Holy Spirit allowed the Gospel to be heard in many languages. Amazing.

Let's step out of the box and stretch our thoughts a little bit to see how that may apply within the framework of our concern. While there's one Holy Spirit, there's diversity within the body of Christ, the ear of the soul and the language the soul understands. It isn't a language you can study or learn. It's language that emanates from your being. Just as teaching styles have been adapted to address different learning styles, so God created you, unique in your language to resonate with the diversity of his hearers. Authenticity is your divine responsibility to God, yourself, and for the sake of others whom you're meticulously designed to serve.

There are those who will only hear the message of the Gospel in the language of your speech, your voice. Not talking about the language of a nationality (African, French, German, …) but your language, that which is filtered through the wisdom gleaned from the testimony of your life journey. Your voice doesn't change the story; it doesn't change the truth but it changes how the story is told. It may include passion and compassion not experienced by others, yet which makes the story audible to someone who otherwise couldn't hear it. If you're a copycat, then all those whom you were created to bless will be robbed of what was meant for them. God supplies every need. Your voice is the supply of someone's need.

Your voice is the supply of someone's need

There's no one else like you. There's a musical sound in you that is your own. A rhythm that emanates from your soul. A melody in the lyrics of your speech. The rhythm, the melody, and the lyrics create a symphonic language that is uniquely yours. It takes an emotionally secure, spiritually mature person to hear and appreciate their symphony and say within, I like the song born in my soul. When you hear it, that's when you've heard your own voice.

Let's revisit the question, "Do I know my own mind?" from the perspective of what it has to do with preaching. A question not to be answered hastily. The question isn't to suggest that you preach your own opinion, but to examine how you process the truths that lie before you and how you interpret matters in a time of change, in a world of broad exposure and intellectual access.

Volumes can be written on how times have changed; how the world has changed. Norms, values, beliefs, rules, ideologies, philosophies, continue to be challenged more quickly and dramatically than ever in the history of humanity. There is the thought, however, that things and people have not changed all that much. Cyberspace has created a global community exposing you to information previously unavailable. As a global citizen, you're exposed to information that sharpens your insight, expands your world view, and your thinking. That which existed without your knowledge is now in your personal space. You can no longer rest in the comfort of limited thoughts, experiences, and opinions, regurgitating what you've heard.

The information super highway has changed and challenged our reality on every level. Every belief is confronted and tested. The world will never be the same, and that's exciting. With all the change, however, the preacher is called to proclaim an unchanged Gospel in a language that speaks its relevance to a world that is different in ways unfamiliar to our experience. The prevailing thought or interpretations through the grid from years gone by may be too narrow for the larger landscape in which you now live. They may or may not be relevant or absolute in this regard: It may be conclusive based on the information available in a time and a particular social location. Yes, truth is what it is and does not change, but, revelation is God's prerogative. Be cautious of the arrogance to believe that in the breadth of your finite thinking; in the nanosecond of time you occupy in eternity, that you hold the complete volume of eternal truth. As time peels back layers of reality, a larger view brings greater light. That which was previously thought to be conclusive gives way to new considerations, new thoughts revelatory of a bigger and greater God.

You are called to a specific moment in history. You weren't born or called in the horse and buggy day, or the days of only snail mail and 10 cents per call phone booths on the street. You're called in the age of technology. Silicon Valley has given the world tools never imagined even 20 years ago. The Internet has made it possible to experience new horizons, exposed diversity and challenges to faith and Christian values. That alone is God pealing back more layers of himself for you to experience. You can no longer relax in the comfort zone of neighborhood thinking; rest in the familiarity of limited thoughts, experiences, and opinions. The world is at your doorstep, in your living room, on the smart devices your children hold in their hands and the social networks with which no one can keep up. You're called to reach a generation that no longer lives in the neighborhood but the world. Called in this generation to the awareness of the globalism and all the implications and applications. The information super highway has changed and challenged our reality on every level. Every belief is challenged and tested. The world will never be the same. Things once hidden are now vying to be normative. What someone else thought about something may not be what resonates in that place where God speaks in your spirit.

You are trusted with the truth in the time in which you live. Congregations that sit before you aren't the congregations of "Ozzie & Harriet" or "Father Knows Best." of yester year. Education, information and social location, change thinking. No, you're not called to change the truth but to give it a voice that's comprehensible. Examine and re-examine the challenges before you. It's not the message that needs to be changed because truth endures through all generations, but the voice God requires in such a time as this may be different. If may be yours.

In the pursuit of your own voice, do you have the courage to accept the challenges to the things you've believed in and see what's left standing? There may be a difference in what you've been preaching when you were not in your authentic self. Have you the courage to give your own thoughts a second thought? Think about it.

Who do people say that I am?

Jesus and his disciples left Galilee and went up to the villages near Caesarea Philippi. As they were walking along, he asked them, "Who do people say I am?" Mark 8:27 NLT

Departing from the traditional interpretation of this scripture and using Jesus' question to illustrate a thought that can be extracted as a sub context, Jesus wasn't asking about the "buzz." He knew the people were talking about him, what they'd witnessed, what they'd heard and what they'd experienced. You can imagine with all he'd done; he would wonder how that translated in the people's minds. Were they "getting it?" He wasn't asking about what they thought of his deeds. He asked is disciples specifically not "what," but "who" the people were saying he was. Then he asked an even more poignant question, "Who do YOU say that I am?"

When Jesus was with the multitudes in the villages and on the outskirts of the cities he was healing and teaching. That was the perception of him some of the people had; healer, teacher. He was with his disciples day and night. They knew him up close and personal. He was asking if there was harmony between the man the people saw and the man the disciples knew; between his public persona and the man he was in his personal circle. Perhaps he was more concerned about who the disciples thought he was. Nevertheless, his question poses a sub context: Is everyone seeing the same thing? It takes a bit of courage to go there. Can people trust who/what they see? Authenticity is a matter of integrity. Dare to think about it and ask yourself some questions. Who am I? Am I projecting my authentic self or a copy of someone else? Am I coming across the way I hope that I am?

To be your authentic self you must be well acquainted with your-self, and accept yourself as a product of God's handiwork; perfections and perfect imperfections. An insecure person with difficulty accepting him/herself, with a flawed sense of self-worth and unhealed wounds cannot be a servant else they will use and abuse the people of God to meet their own needs. A person dissatisfied with their self will try to find someone else to be.

> Who do people say you are? Can they trust what they see?

Consider spiritual gifts within the framework of this discussion. Think of them in terms of being a part of a larger whole, the big picture of God's human tapestry. Positioning yourself in that framework will open your eyes as to how and where you fit in. Think of yourself in practical terms; your personality, habits, tendencies, attitudes, etc. What excites you and motivates you? What makes your heart sing? You are who you are. God created you so you're in his plan. He can use you if you are willing to be your authentic self.

PRAYERFULLY PONDER

1. What's unique about you?

_____

_____

_____

_____

_____

2. What are you known for?

_____

_____

_____

_____

_____

3. What are your spiritual gifts? How do you use them?

_____

_____

_____

_____

_____

Pray for my soul. *More things are wrought by prayer*
Than this world dreams of. Wherefore, let thy voice
Rise like a fountain for me night and day.
For what are people better than sheep or goats
That nourish a blind life within the brain,
If, knowing God, they lift not hands of prayer
Both for themselves and those who call them friends?
For so the whole round earth is every way
Bound by gold chains about the feet of God

-   - Alfred, Lord Tennyson

THE 3ᴿᴰ COMMANDMENT

THOU SHALL LINK TO THE CLOUD

& MAKE HEAVEN YOUR HOMEPAGE. CREATE an account (a relationship with Jesus), and Stay Logged In. You need WIFI (Word Inspired Faith Ignited) that powers your connectivity to the Cloud. Mentally Hyperlink positive scriptures. Bookmark every blessing for quick recall when you need them. The Holy Spirit is your data. Without WIFI you have limited data; with WIFI you have access to unlimited data. Choose the plan that's right for you.

Prayer is the life blood of an anointed preaching ministry. So fundamental that prayer metaphors are everywhere. The wind tunnel of the Ruach. The flight path of the anointing. The raceway of divine power. Each metaphor, a channel. Consider this metaphor that may be more familiar, the train track for prayer. The power, anointing, insight, spirit sight, boldness you need to be strong in your call comes down on the track of prayer you lay. Imagine every prayer is a railroad tie. You lay the tracks that allow the power, healing, and blessings of every kind to get to their destinations.

Your track is only as strong as the quality of your railroad ties and the care you take in laying each one. Just as with physical railroad tracks, regular maintenance is required to make sure the train can get to its destination without incidents, interruptions or delays, so it is in the spirit realm with prayer. Tracks of prayer need regular attention to be strong enough to sustain the power that needs to come down the track. The more chaotic the world, the more power needed and the stronger the track needs to be.

Imagine people waiting for the train with the cargo of blessings they need coming down your track. Imagine even yourself waiting. Is there enough track for the train to come down? Is the track in good repair, strong enough such that the powerful train of blessings can come down or is the track weak and the train has to move slowly? People are waiting for the train coming in on your tracks. If your tracks are weak and raggedy, that could cause delays. A disciplined prayer life keeps your tracks in good repair; keeps them well-oiled for smooth locomotion.

A disciplined behavior of any kind, eating, exercise, study, reading, resting, etc. takes time to establish and purposeful action to maintain. Isn't it interesting how easy it is to develop a bad habit and tough to maintain a good one? There's so much to do and so little time. You're called to preach but called amid the demands of life which do not diminish just because there's a call on your life. You still must go to work and be your best. You still must plan and prepare meals, do laundry, feed the cat on time, walk the dog twice and sing to the goldfish. Is there any time left for yourself? Is there enough time left to cultivate and nurture the relationship with God that your soul desires? Only you can answer that question, and you must answer the question – and the sooner the better. Time management isn't church jargon. It doesn't come up in Sunday School or bible study. But, beloved, it's a make or break thing. If you don't manage your time you'll always find yourself trying to find time to pray; trying to find time to get it in, rushing to get a quick prayer in just before preaching time and hope that God responds so you won't embarrass him or yourself by being that sounding brass and tinkling symbol. Or worse yet, walk away from the mic with that sick feeling that comes from knowing you didn't do your best.

Design your prayer life in a way that works for you, early morning before the sun rises and the busyness of the day prevails upon your mind, or evening after the rush of life has settled. Choose a time that best fits your lifestyle and be consistent. Consistency is essential. You can imagine, if you'd like, that being consistent allows God to know what time to expect you to enter into his gates with thanks giving and into his courts with praise. The truth is consistency is more vital for your spiritual health than it is for God. He already knows when to expect your presence. Whether random or regular, God already knows your ETA (exact time of arrival) in the throne room of God. It isn't about keeping God waiting and hoping that today you'll come. It's about your need to be there; to be in the presence of the one who refuels your engine, renews your strength, restores your joy and puts back together the broken pieces that life has caused. It's about being in the presence of the one who clarifies your vision, wipes your tears, and encourages you forward when weariness calls you back. Maintaining consistency says being in the presence of God is a priority. You don't need a book or seminar to tell you how to set your priorities. You know what the priorities are in your life.

Your spirit that so depends on fresh anointing is stronger with a consistent personal prayer meeting. Strength and power[u] are drawn from the Holy Spirit, and delighting in the presence of God. Delighting in God's presence is just being happy to be there. Beloved, you can't fake the power necessary for effective preaching; and you can't fake the anointing necessary for power. Some think preaching with power and authority is preaching with a loud voice and a commanding presence. You can fool some people with that for a while, but in the fullness of time,

[u] Psalm 62:11

your emptiness will show. When the anointing is present and the Word of God goes forth, promises in the Word manifest in the lives of the people; sometimes on the spot, other times over time. A steady expression of a fake anointing time after time, week after week, month after month will yield nothing. Lives don't change, members don't remain, no power, no healing, no evidence of God. Just the "Whoop[v]" and I say this respectfully, the anointing isn't in the whoop. If you don't know what the whoop is, don't worry about it. That probably means you don't do it.

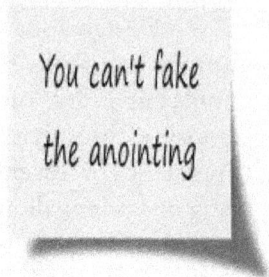

> You can't fake the anointing

To preach the Word of God with power and authority you must begin with a relationship with the one who is/and has the power and authority, who'll anoint you with more of himself as you grow in that relationship through prayer.

Have Regular Face Time with God

There are days when sermon fodder just drops into your spirit; a scripture, scenery, a piece of art, a song, a conversation, an encounter. It's like God has the universe speaking to you on his behalf. You pause in prayer asking God to give you the message he wants to convey and suddenly you can make three sermons out of just one thought. GLORY!!! Other days the well is dry. You feel so desperate that you'll crack open a Chinese fortune cookie for a motivating thought. Maybe you've been too busy answering everyone's call, meeting everyone else's needs and your spirit is just simply exhausted. The dry, barren and empty times are those when the Spirit of God draws you to green

---

[v] A vocal signature style sermon celebration in the African American preaching tradition

pastures, desiring to lead you beside the still waters so that he can restore your soul.[w]

You may be of the tradition that uses the lectionary as common practice. Even with the Lectionary you can still be in a dry place where there's no meat on the bones. Unfortunately, those times have no regular schedule. You can't plan your vacation time around them. The Bible speaks of principalities[x] and powers and spiritual wickedness in high places.[y] A principality as it relates to our interest here is an order of angels, transcending or superior to the physical world in conflict with God. There's a spirit realm around you that you can't see. So, what you're dealing with is a small group of entities with limited power that can mess up things in a big way if you don't protect yourself using the greater power, the Holy Spirit, through the powerful medium of prayer.

You don't go through the day thinking about being in active warfare and under attack unless something's going wrong, plans didn't work out, a loved one dies, a disease comes, kids acting crazy, ministry's ineffective, membership isn't growing, church is **Pray for 20/20 vision in the spirit realm** dying, … Prayer becomes an intense concern in difficult times. In the heat of the battle prayers are effective. You cut through the fluff in battle ground prayer. The fact is, spiritual warfare is going on 24/7. That's real time, right now time. Praying real time is praying without ceasing.[z] Even when you're in a good space and blessings are overtaking you, put a reminder on your smart phone that there's a plot against you and the work of your

---

[w] Psalm 23
[x] Principalities: territories, countries, domains within a larger kingdom or government
[y] Ephesians 6:12
[z] I Thessalonians 5:17

call. Don't take your eye off the ball. Don't let your guard down. Amid your praise and thanksgiving, pray for protection against what you can't see. Ask for wisdom to handle the onslaught yet to come.

This isn't to suggest that a disciplined prayer life is an insurance policy against dry times. It is not. But it is an assurance and reassurance as you step up to the sacred desk that the Holy Spirit will do his job in spite of how you feel. A disciplined prayer life keeps your storehouse of assurance filled. There's power in the Name of Jesus and the Holy Spirit releases that power as you spend time in the presence of God.

Pray Wisely

In 2nd Chronicles 1, Solomon, is in a good place. He was walking in God's promise to David that his son would be his successor as King of Israel, a very large kingdom. He had thousands of commanders and hundreds of judges under his leadership. He was a worshiper, wealthy, well liked, and had the favor of God. When God appeared to Solomon asking him what he would ask of him, Solomon did three things:

1. He acknowledged God's great mercy and lovingkindness toward his father, David. (Past)

2. He acknowledged that God had kept his promise to make him successor to the throne, entrusted with the leadership of the great number of people who belonged to God. (Present)

3. He asked for wisdom and knowledge to lead God's people justly. (Future)

Clearly God was impressed with Solomon beyond the fact that he was David's son. Solomon's character was reflected in his prayer. God not only granted the wisdom and knowledge Solomon asked for, but riches, possessions, and honor, such as none of the kings who were before him or after him. Solomon prayed in the good times and God made provisions for his future. The point is to be disciplined in your prayer life and to pray wise prayers.

Auto Correct

Of course, we don't always know what to pray for as we should. At times, our judgment may be cloudy, our flesh may be in the way. Maybe our best understanding falls short of the will of God. God created a patch for that. Better yet, he designed Auto Correct. The Holy Spirit will auto correct your prayers.[aa]

Three Things to Pray for:

1.   A Teachable Spirit

A teachable spirit is priceless. It's benefit to you, it's worth to those with and for whom you work and serve, is beyond measure. Not possessed by everyone; unnecessary on the path of "get over;" or the road to mediocrity. It is, however, a non-negotiable characteristic necessary to walk the path to excellence. We don't come to the call ready-made, ready to hit the ground running. We come to be developed, honed, and perfected. You need to be open and ready for the process.

A person with a teachable spirit can be taught, and is receptive to wise counsel without being defensive or feeling belittled. Someone may ask them to do something in ministry that others would feel is beneath them (teach bible study at a nursing home, be involved in the youth ministry, go door to door with the evangelism team, …). The person with the teachable spirit doesn't define themselves by what they're asked to do. Instead they see it as an opportunity

[aa] Romans 8:26-28

to learn and take from the experience that which will give them what they need for the future. One with a teachable spirit can be trusted to represent the king among kings. They can be trusted to take to the experience what they've been taught and bring back what they've learned. God can pour himself into a teachable spirit and know the result will reflect himself.

God has a purpose for your life. He didn't just get a good idea and then decide to call you to make it happen. He predestined you before the foundation of the world. He saw and fashioned you in your mother's womb. The Holy Spirit imparted in you the gifts you'd need to fulfill God's purpose in your life. He designs experiences for your growth. He sends people in your life to groom you, help you to interpret your experiences, and give you the wisdom you need to go forward in excellence. Others may have a different view or approach to something, but diversity can add dimensions to our own realization of truth. Seldom can we perceive a situation in its entirety. Others can offer the benefit of new approaches that will expand our understanding and comprehension.

A person with a teachable spirit is a person who's willing to listen. They aren't simply being silent while another is speaking and waiting their turn to speak. They listen to hear and understand what's being said, believing the other person is sharing more than their own opinions, but the wisdom poured into them from the experiences of their life and the lives of others who have poured into them.

Conversely, a person with an unteachable spirit is a "know it all." The "know it all," knows it all, and no one likes a "know it all." Their receptors are clogged with "my way" residue and the dregs of self-aggrandizement. There's nothing you can teach them because they know it all. There's no openness to be enriched by others. Any leader would prefer a less gifted person with a teachable spirit than a highly-gifted person who can't take direction and correction. Better to be less gifted with a teachable spirit then to be a highly gifted "know it all." An unteachable spirit will cause you to miss God's best.

Five Characteristics of a Teachable Spirit:

1. Willingness to receive wise counsel; an openness to suggestions and new ideas

2. Welcomes the consideration of alternative thoughts and different points of view

3. Receptiveness to direction from more experienced others

4. Views correction as a path to the greater possibility

5. Keeps the ego healthy

2. A Mentor

There are people whom you admire, smart people, successful people, people at the top of their game in their professions. Perhaps they're even accessible. Secular wisdom offers many "how to's" in choosing a mentor; what to look for, things to consider, etc. Some even say you don't choose your mentor, but that your mentor chooses you. The rules, however, in the Kingdom realm are different. You don't choose your mentor; God chooses your mentor. He created you with a purpose in mind. He knows what it will take to get you to your purpose. He'll bring the right people at the right time to get you to your destiny. It's a match made in heaven and orchestrated by the Holy Spirit on earth. No matter how incredibly gifted you may be, you cannot go it alone. Moses had Jethro,[bb] Samuel had

---

[bb] Exodus 18: 1, 6-27

Eli,[cc] Elisha had Elijah,[dd] Ruth had Naomi,[ee] Mary had Elizbeth,[ff] Paul had Barnabus,[gg] to name only a few.

The Kingdom of God has not been awaiting your arrival. Others have come this way before you. This is simply your time in the plan of God. You don't know how long your time will be and surely you want it to be the best it can be. Open your ears to hear the experiences of others. A mentor will share their experiences as well as what they've observed. Open your heart to know wisdom. A true mentor will share from a heart of love for the call and for those in the call. Open your mind to thoughts other than your own. A mentor will encourage you in the good times, in the rough times, and at all times. A mentor will undergird you in prayer, affirm and find joy in the work of God in you without envy or jealousy.

Pray for God to send a mentor and that you'll recognize and receive them; a person whose wisdom you trust; in whose counsel, you have confidence; whose journey you respect; who's seasoned in the same or similar call; a person who can keep you grounded and help you to keep your head on straight.

3.   A Micah Mindset (*Micah 6:8 (MSG)*

But he's already made it plain how to live, what to do, what God is looking for in men and women. It's quite simple: Do what is fair and just to your neighbor, be compassionate and loyal in your love, and don't take yourself too seriously — take God seriously.

Because it's up front and highly visible, the ministry of preaching is viewed as a lofty calling and preachers often put on

---

[cc] 1 Samuel 3
[dd] 2 Kings
[ee] Ruth 1:7-18; Ruth 2:17-3:6; Ruth 4:13-17
[ff] Luke 1: 39–56
[gg] Acts 9, 11; Acts 9: 26-31; Acts 11:19-26; Acts 14:1-3

a pedestal. Fight that with all your might. You can't really change the perceptions people have. Often their perceptions are reflections of what they need. But you can control yourself. Never lose sight of your humanity. Hold onto your sense of compassion and mercy. Ruthlessly fight the temptation to be judgmental.[hh]

In the poem "If" by Rudyard Kipling he says walk with kings but don't lose the common touch. (paraphrase). Despite your call be able to step down from your seat at the head table and sit with someone who's seated alone. Speak up for those who have no voice. Use your influence to make right things happen.

There are jobs, positions, callings that will have you seated at the king's table but always remember how you got there. You're there because God opened doors for you to be there. You're there because God caused you to be favored in the sight of the powers that be so that you can wisely speak truth to power with prudence. You're there because he trusts you to speak fairly, justly, and compassionately from a heart of mercy, on behalf of his people unconditionally loved and valued. He trusts you to represent him among kings and queens. He sets you in high places so that you can have a better view of the landscape of life, the bigger picture, the long view which allows you to see the intersection of love and truth and to lift the Word of God off the page in a way that others will only know through your ministry.

[hh] Galatians 6:1

Is Your Spirit Teachable?	Yes ✓	No ✓
1. Do you have a willingness to receive wise counsel w/o feeling defensive?		
2. Are you open and receptive to suggestions and new ideas?		
3. Do you welcome the consideration of alternative thoughts and differing points of view (different from your own)?		
4. Are you receptive to direction from more experienced others?		
5. Do you view correction as a path to the greater possibilities?		
6. Do you feel appreciative when someone tries to give you advice?		
7. Do you feel comfortable when someone questions the direction in which you're going?		
8. When someone points out an inconsistency, do you shift into explain mode?		
9. Are you proactive when it comes to training, self-development, and getting the information you need?		
10. Do you implement and act on the ideas and principles you receive?		

PRAYERFULLY PONDER

1. What's the most important area of your ministry that needs prayer?

_____

_____

_____

_____

2. List at least five reasons to have a mentor.

_____

_____

_____

_____

_____

3. What are the three main principles in Micah 6:8?

_____

_____

_____

_____

The Eagle Who Thought He Was a Chicken

A baby eagle became orphaned when something happened to his parents. He glided down to the ground from his nest but was not yet able to fly. A man picked him up, took him to a farmer and said, "This is a special kind of barnyard chicken that will grow up big." The farmer said, "Don't look like no barnyard chicken to me." "Oh yes, it is. You will be glad to own it." The farmer took the baby eagle and placed it with his chickens.

The baby eagle learned to imitate the chickens. He could scratch the ground for grubs and worms too. He grew up thinking he was a chicken.

Then one day an eagle flew over the barnyard. The eagle looked up and wondered, "What kind of animal is that? How graceful, powerful, and free it is." Then he asked another chicken, "What is that?" The chicken replied, "Oh, that is an eagle. But don't worry yourself about that. You will never be able to fly like that."

And the eagle went back to scratching the ground. He continued to behave like the chicken he thought he was. Finally, he died, never knowing the grand life that could have been his.

THE 4TH COMMANDMENT

THOU SHALL WISELY CHOOSE
THINE INNER CIRCLE

B IRDS OF A FEATHER FLOCK TOGETHER. When you look around and take inventory of the birds in your flock, you might be tempted to dispute that truism, but before you do, check your feathers. There's something about those in your circle, some commonality, whether obvious or subtle, that attracts them to you and you to them. Take a moment to digest that. It happens without any effort at all; people stay in their comfort zone, around people with whom they're familiar and have much in common. Billionaires Warren Buffett and Bill Gates are friends; Oprah Winfrey and Gayle King are friends. No disrespect or offense intended, but when did you last have lunch with T.D. Jakes or Joyce Meyer and who else in your circle was there? People gravitate toward others who are likeminded, in same or similar professions, socio-economic location, share similar philosophies, etc.

It's a great thing to have family and friends in your circle. There's a feeling of security with the familiar and there's a level of nurture that only the familiar can give. Nevertheless, receive this caution. Your comfort zone is fertile ground for the roots of mediocrity to grow deep and strong. Your comfort zone is just that, the place where you're comfortable. You know the rhythm of the environment, what's expected of you and what you can expect from others. No one pushes you to go higher because average becomes the norm and people become complacent in the usual. No one rocks the boat; no one challenges you to take a half step above the ordinary because when you do, that raises the bar for everyone. Many people are just fine operating at the level of mediocrity. Perhaps not you. Maybe you have more in your reservoir but in your comfort zone more isn't needed. It's a rut and you need to get out of it.

That's what this Fourth Commandment is about, your world, your circle, more specifically, your inner circle. Time passes without notice. When you live in the complacency of ordinariness your spirit becomes lethargic, curiosity finds no energy and creativity finds no egress. The new things God has for you to bring to the world becomes someone else's assignment.

If you confine yourself to a small, homogeneous environment, you'll restrict your growth to the level of your self-imposed limitations and that of those around you. Jesus didn't do that. Think about it. Think about the different places he went and different people he encountered and his interaction with them. Just that alone speaks volumes about the model of ministry he set forth. A small world, a myopic world view, only yields a recycling of the same thoughts, ideas, opinions, and interpretations. Complacency allows you to regurgitate what you've heard unedited. You need to expand your circle to include others who can stimulate your growth. Build relationships with creative thinkers. Others who, regardless of age, are excited about the journey of life, new things to discover, different ideas to explore. Expand your sphere of

> A small world view recycles the same thoughts, ideas, opinions and interpretations

influence to enrich your life, stimulate personal, intellectual, creative, professional, and spiritual growth, not just for yourself but for the people God has called you to feed and the people in your life that matter.

How do you do that? Have conversations with people who may think a little differently, who aren't in the same church or the same denomination. The internet and social network are great tools if you use them properly. Check out preachers you wouldn't ordinarily listen to, preachers from around the world. You don't have to join their church, denomination, or reformation; just check out what God is doing beyond your own little world. There's an old hymn that says, "The Lord will make a way somehow." If you want to be in a bigger space in ministry, the Lord will make a way somehow. He'll bring the right people into your sphere. Your job is to receive them and make room for the unfolding revelations of God's self in your ministry.

The Tabula Rasa (blank slate) theory of human development, credited to English philosopher, John Locke and Swiss philosopher Jean-Jacques Rousseau, was first documented in the late 17th and early 18th centuries. The theory says that humans are born with no knowledge, an empty mind, completely free of any predisposition or vulnerabilities, and that knowledge from experience and the effects of the environment shape and define who a person becomes. Therefore, a person has no identity until after birth.

We now know, of course, that isn't true. Mothers feel the temperament of the baby while they're still in the womb especially in the last trimester. Babies tend to have a sleep pattern while still in the womb. We can see little personalities in babies almost immediately after birth. Some are calm, others are fussy. Some respond with a smile and baby babble only weeks after birth. Others seem to ignore any efforts to get a response from them. The Bible teaches that we were known by God before the foundation of the world, that he breathed himself into us, so we were not born blank slates. However, the part of the theory that's of interest is the idea that external influences have such strong power in shaping and molding lives. Through associations you form your world view, you get to know yourself better. As you broaden the boundaries of your world you see more of yourself and you see more of God. That can be frightening to a person who needs to see God as familiar and predictable, his ways logically explainable, in a nice neat little box. The first step to broadening your sphere of influence is allowing yourself to become comfortable with ambiguity; be okay with being unable to explain everything that has to do with God. Be okay with something or someone God may bring into your world that may seem like an unlikely friend. The person may be of a different race, a different socio-economic level. God is eternal. He cannot be contained. He cannot be fully known. The more you know of him the more there is to know. You cannot drain the well of who God is so **stretch, stretch, stretch** yourself to see more. As you see more and allow God to do more in your life, he will bring people into your life you may never have reached out to. He knows a lot of people, he has a bigger network, and he knows who to send to impact your life for an amazing future.

> As you broaden the boundaries of your world, you see more of God

If you have a gnawing, unrest inside, a feeling that says, "There's got to be more to life than this, more to ministry than this," then that's the Holy Spirit putting the little eagle's view of the sky in your spirit, telling you that there is more. If you want to go to where there's more, then you need to leave the chickens and develop a network of eagles. A network that transcends where you are now. This isn't to suggest that you cut your family ties or shun your lifelong friends. It simply means you need to do some work in your garden, perhaps transplant some flowers. Enlarge your territory. Open yourself to relationships with people who have big ideas, big dreams, ambitious plans, meaningful purposes; people who generate the energy off which others can feed; energy that invigorates you to achieve your goals. New flowers in your garden don't have to be the same. They don't have to be preachers to be in your inner circle. There is so much to be learned as others share their gifts and the wisdom of their experiences. If you're the smartest one in your circle, then your circle is of very little meaningful benefit. Boring. Just a recycling of the same old conversations and the same old points of view. You'll never grow in that circle and you'll never be happy there. Ask yourself if you have the need to be the smartest one in your group. If your answer is "yes," then you need a therapist. Hang up your collar until you can get your head on straight.

What is an inner circle?

Let's start with an understanding of your inner circle. Look at the visual illustration on the next page. That's "you" standing in the middle. The circle of people closest to you is your inner circle, your closest group of friends. There may or may not be family members in your inner circle. These are they whom you reach out to first when you want to make certain your new idea makes sense. These are the ones you call when you have a mountain in front of you that needs to be moved. These are the friends whose advice you trust. Your inner circle are the people who are up close and personal, who know your hopes and dreams, your goals, and visions. They know your fears and weaknesses. They want your highest good and they want you to make it. Your inner circle are your champions, your protectors. They celebrate your good and cover your bad.

The next circle of people is your outer circle. These may be family, neighbors, or associates. That which differentiates inner circle friends from outer circle friends is the depth of friendship. There are those in your outer circle who you may call "friend," but you can't share your deepest goals and visions. You

Your Inner Circle   Your Outer Circle

know they won't understand. Those in your outer circle may want the best for you but they can't help you get there. Perhaps their world view is too small. Perhaps they have limited ability to see. Some people just like things to remain the same.

"Who's Who" in your Inner Circle?

Jim Rohm, personal development expert, says, "We're the combined average of those we spend most of our time with." Now, that's reveille, your bugle call, your trumpet call, your loud wake-up call. The people you're spending your time with may be nice, sweet people in many ways but they may not be the picture you envision of yourself.

You may be like the eagle in the story. He was acting like the chickens because there were only chickens in his inner circle. But there was something on the inside that knew he was more than a chicken. Chickens don't fly and they don't want to. You need to be deliberate and strategic in choosing your inner circle friends. If you want to fly, if you believe you can fly, you need to be around people who want to fly. People who have flown, who've seen life from a higher vantage point.

Who's who in your inner circle matters. It's so important that you choose wisely those who comprise that space in your world. You're judged by the company you keep. The people who are consistently around you, in many ways, define the perception of who you are and the heights to which you will go. So, who's who in your inner circle?

> You will never rise
> any higher than
> the circle around you

How does one get to occupy the coveted position of being a part of your inner circle? Jesus had thousands of followers, but he chose twelve disciples. It wasn't whosoever came along could come along. He carefully chose the twelve which strongly suggests that you give attention to who's in your outer circle as well as your inner circle. Of the twelve there were only three in his inner circle, Peter, James and John. They were the ones with whom he shared his most personal thoughts, plans and ideas. They were the ones with whom he shared intimate moments of prayer, pain and disappointment. What qualified them to be his inner circle? Just because a person is related to you, lives in your neighborhood, or has known you for a long time, doesn't qualify them to be a part of your inner circle. You may love someone dearly but that doesn't qualify them to be a part of your inner circle. It isn't selfish or snobbish to hold the view that what a person brings to your life experience now and potentially, positions them to be considered a candidate for your inner circle. This is your life and you're responsible to take care of it wisely.

What do they bring? Everyone has baggage. The fact that a person has lived past the womb means they have baggage. If you're inviting someone into the inner circle on your life journey, you need to check their bags; see what experiences they're bringing. They may seem like a good fit, but as much as possible, you want to get a look at their inner circle to see who they're bringing with them. Your friend may have a friend that isn't your friend. Your friend may have associates you don't see. Though they're invisible to you, you may feel their presence and influence channeled through your friend. Influence via association is a fact you cannot control but you can be aware of it as much as possible. Do a baggage check.

Do Baggage Check

The people you have around you significantly influence your progress. That which is around you rubs off on you. If you spend time with jealous, critical, unhappy people, you'll soon become the same. You need to be in the right mix. That may require you to prune off relationships that don't add anything to your life. You can't hang around chickens and hope to fly with eagles. In other words, don't spend your time with people who are unmotivated, sloppy and going nowhere; people without goals and dreams. Don't spend your time with people who are undisciplined, who have no focus, for whom mediocrity is the norm. They may have a good heart. They may not be bad people. They're just not good for you.

There's much written about the personality traits, character, and characteristics that you should look for in candidates for your inner circle. At the top of the list is to have people of strong unshakeable faith and a deeply rooted positive attitude. Invite people who speak positively about things; who have good things to say about others; who see great possibilities. The Bible has much to say about speech and the power of the spoken word. Death and life are in the power of the tongue. You need people who speak life into your life and life into the atmosphere. Words spoken reflect what's in the heart. Positive words are life giving and have the power of encouragement.

Listen to their speech; people reveal themselves in their conversations.

- Do they send out positive energy into the atmosphere?
- Do they send out praise for who God is, what he's done, and what he's capable of?
- Do they have an Ephesians 3:20 conversation?

You need people in your inner circle who know and believe the Word of God and have faith in his promises; people who so exhaust themselves with the positive that they are too tired to be negative. You can always find people who will play "the devil's advocate." You don't need that. The devil doesn't need any more advocates; he has an army of his own. You need people who are likeminded in that they believe in themselves, believe in you, and have big vision and know God is bigger than any circumstance, any obstacle or any vision he's placed in your heart.

The Second Ending To The Eagle's Story

He looked up and flew with the eagles.

How will your story end?

Will you stay on the ground clucking with chickens, or will you look up, spread your powerful wings, and fly with the eagles?

	Vet Your Inner Circle	Yes ✓	No ✓
1.	Do they inspire you to stretch yourself beyond your comfort zone?		
2.	Do they encourage you to think bigger, try new things, consider new ideas and fresh perspectives?		
3.	Do they challenge you to think outside of the box?		
4.	Do they add value to your life? If yes, how?		
5.	Do they have relationships with champions?		
6.	Do they encourage you to be your best self?		
8.	Do they hold you to the goals you've set for yourself? (Accountability partnership)		
9.	Have you checked their bags?		
10.	How do they speak of people close to them? (Circle one)	+	-

PRAYERFULLY PONDER

Yes or No answers only get your thinking started. Think deeper:

1. On a separate sheet of paper, list the people in your inner circle, and what they do for a living. Are they moving forward or have they been in the same position for years?

2. What have you done as a result of their encouragement to stretch yourself beyond your comfort zone?

3. What new things or new ideas have been a result of their encouragement?

4. How have they encouraged you to think more broadly? If so, how?

5. How do they add value to your life? How are you better because of them?

6. Who are the encouraging and influential people in their lives?

7. What are their visions and goals for their life?

"If you know the enemy and know yourself, you need not fear the result of a hundred battles. If you know yourself but not the enemy, for every victory gained you will also suffer a defeat. If you know neither the enemy nor yourself, you will succumb in every battle."

— Sun Tzu, The Art of War

THE 5TH COMMANDMENT

THOU SHALL FLEE JEALOUSY & ENVY

EET THE INFAMOUS TWIN DEMONS, Jealousy and Envy. They travel together, look alike, often behave alike, people confuse them, but make no mistake. They're different. It's well worth your time to know them and clearly recognize the distinct difference between the two because left unleashed these two emotions are very formidable enemies, skillfully stealth in taking down kings and queens, destroying nations and killing hopes and dreams without shedding one drop of blood, although they have been known to be the impetus behind malicious criminal behavior, even murder. Because this book is for preachers, the two concepts are confined within the context of church life, but think not for a moment they behave differently in the Kingdom of God than in the natural world. They'll sucker punch anyone regardless of where they are or who they are.

In the fifth chapter of the first letter that bears his name, Peter issues a wake-up call using two strong words, sober and vigilant. To be sober is to be clear minded and free from the influence of anything mind altering. Vigilant is to be watchful and cautious. You need to be sober and vigilant at all times in this call. Use your sanctified imagination and envision twin lions, Envy and Jealousy, stalking you day and night. The surest path to defeat in any adversarial situation is to underestimate your enemy. Don't make that mistake with these two. Envy and jealousy are emotions, deceptively similar but different. In one way, they are even each other's opposite: envy is evoked when someone has something good that you want, jealousy when you have something good that you believe someone else wants to have. Envy involves a longing for what you don't have. If you crave a mega church like Bishop Awesome, you're envious of Bishop Awesome. If you're upset about losing your members to him, you're jealous. Emotions are powerful. With equal dexterity, they can motivate you to greatness with enthusiasm or to destruction with the ease and precision of a lion's powerful swipe.

Both these emotions lie within the flesh to a greater or lesser degree. The frequency and intensity of their appearance is primarily contingent upon individual personality, temperament, the way one looks at the world, and spiritual maturity. While the call to preach is a divine call, it falls upon the human vessel, therefore subjecting it to the preacher's internal struggles, the war between the flesh and the spirit which Paul so thoroughly and eloquently describes in Romans 12:14-24. It's important to understand from two vantage points and multiple perspectives how envy and jealousy operate. You can be jealous or envious, or the object of someone's jealousy or envy. Both are considered here.

ENVY

To feel envious of someone, you need to compare yourself to that person. You can envy someone's intelligence, good looks, social position, or relationship with a person. In each of these cases, you determine that the other person is better off than you, and that you would want that good thing for yourself. Psychologists suggest there are two types of envy: Benign Envy and Malicious Envy.

When You Envy Others (Benign Envy: The Safe Zone)

Benign envy is the kind which raises you up rather than making you want to pull the other person down. It carries a positive connotation, a type of emotional stimulus that moves the person to aspire to be as good in whatever way as the object of their envy. It can be used to express a desire to equal another in achievement or excellence as in emulation or admiration. In this notion, it's used in a complimentary sense without negative implications. If you say, "I envy the way Rev. Grey can paint a vivid picture as he preaches," this is a positive statement, quite complimentary. If you stop there, you're in the safe zone. There is, however, a very fine line separating the Safe Zone from the Danger Zone.

When You Envy Others (Malicious Envy: The Danger Zone)

We tend to feel malicious envy towards another person if we think their success is undeserved. This is the type that makes us want to strike out at the other person and bring them down a peg or two. Malicious envy also includes the judgment that the other person does not deserve the good thing, so not only do you want to have the object for yourself, you also want the other person to not have it anymore.

Spiritual Gifts, for example, are distributed at the discretion of the Holy Spirit. They are unique to you, customized to your personality, temperament, etc. Your gift is so designed for excellence that if you stir up the gift within you and seek to perfect it, it will operate on the level of excellence for which it was intended. The problem enters in when the system of human evaluation is placed on the spiritual gifts, ascribing a "pyramid of value;" some gifts more valuable than others, therefore, some more desirable than others; or the different administrations of the same gift having differing levels of esteem. Here stalks the lion of malicious envy, a negative emotional influence that ruins a person and his/her mind causing the envious person to blindly want the object of their envy to suffer in some way. They may not want the person to step in front of a bus, but maybe that the sound system die in the middle of their sermon; or let them get stuck in traffic or have a flat causing them to miss the TV taping.

Listen to the conversation between Rev. Green and the Holy Spirit as human value enters the picture in the case of Rev. Green and Rev. White. Notice how Rev. Green was focused on Rev. White's spiritual gift.

Rev. Green: Rev. White has a powerful teaching ministry. Her gift of teaching comes through in her sermons. I wish I had the gift of teaching that Rev. White has. I want to be able to write and deliver teaching sermons.

Holy Spirit: *Teaching is not the gift I've given you. I've given you the gift of healing. How will you use it?*

Rev. Green: Yeah, but I want that gift of teaching. I can do it just as good, if not better than Rev. White.

Holy Spirit: *No you can't do it better. That's not the gift I've given you. I've given you the gift of healing.*

Rev. Green: Yeah, but I want that gift of teaching. I like it better. I know I can do it. Hmmm. In fact, I don't really need Rev. White on staff anymore. I can handle the teaching ministry myself.

When the Holy Spirit called Rev. Green's attention to the gift of healing, Rev. Green never acknowledged his own gift. He recognized that Rev. White was doing a great job so the envy wasn't negative or personally against Rev. White at first. Rev. Green saw something he admired in another preacher. Nothing wrong with that – but he didn't stop there. Sin pushed him into a downward spiral heading straight toward the danger zone. Admiration took a back seat to covetousness, a desire to have what Rev. White had. Finally, instead of recognizing the gift of healing in himself and devising a plan to develop his gift, his plan was to dismiss Rev. White and operate in the gift he wanted instead of the gift he was divinely given. Envy can become negative and personal causing you to enter the danger zone.

You may honestly and without malice admire something another preacher has, a charismatic delivery, abilities, a bigger church, a more supportive congregation. Admiration is honorable. Just be cautious. Envy can turn into a sneaky foe. Admiration can fall prey to envy with covetousness wherein you no longer admire but you desire. Now you have a problem. If you don't bring that feeling under subjection to the Holy Spirit you'll find yourself consumed with the desire and taking steps to get what they have.

Envy doesn't always start out as admiration and desire to emulate. Sometimes envy starts out bad. You've heard of preachers, or perhaps even known one or two who envied the advantages, possessions, notoriety of a colleague, things they desired but lacked. They undermined the ministry of a colleague in order to take it. In the secular world, it's called "back stabbing." In the realm of the ecclesia, there is no holy word for it, it's simply "back stabbing."

When Others Envy You

You may find yourself the focus of another preacher's envy, benign or malicious. Always keep your humility meter fine-tuned through prayerful relationship with God. There are three things you must do when you become aware of envy by a colleague: (1) Keep your head on straight; (2) Commit the matter to prayer; and (3) Keep a safe distance. Take the high road and assume there is no malice intended but you can see how quickly one can go from the safety zone to the danger zone when envy degrades from admiration to covetousness. You have a responsibility to use wisdom to protect yourself. Remember the roaring lion is seeking to devour. Your admirer might suddenly get hungry. You've seen others in the danger zone and you don't want to fall victim to that. To be the object of someone's admiration is affirming and feels nice. Everyone needs affirmation from time to time. Just prayerfully remember that the affirmation is for that which God alone has placed in you. It's the God in you that they see.

JEALOUSY

Jealousy is having the fear that someone is going to take what you have. Jealousy is having the fear and suspicion of losing one's position or situation to someone else. Jealousy has to do with holding on to what you have because you fear that someone else is going to take it away. The operative word is fear. While fear is a vital response to physical and emotional danger, if you didn't feel it, you couldn't protect yourself from legitimate threats, however, fear of loss as defined by jealousy is entirely different. There may or may not be a basis in reality concerning the threat of

> Jealousy is the fear that someone is going to take what you have

the loss, but there is certainly a feeling of resentment and generally describes a sort of emotional rivalry between people. When it comes to jealousy, there is no safety zone. When jealousy appears, it takes you in only one direction. Down. Think about it. If you fear that someone can take something, that describes the feeling of inadequacy. They have the power to take. Jealousy begins to talk to you saying, "You have to fight to keep what you have." Both envy and jealousy breed feelings of inadequacy. When you feel inadequate anger sets in and everyone around you becomes actors in your play.

When You're Jealous of Someone

Real or imagined, you perceive someone has the power to take something away from you. You become distracted from your work and focused on the fight. That person becomes your rival. Even if it's only in your mind, your perception is your reality and you act accordingly. Follow this short hypothetical scenario:

> There's a young, very gifted preacher on your staff. People are excited about him, saying what a good preacher he is, great personality, on and on. They're even saying that you should allow him to preach more often on Sundays, maybe even give him one Sunday a month. You may not recognize it at first but you feel a little something stirring up on the inside. Jealousy is beginning to take root as it did with Saul toward David.
>
> Your imagination gets the better of you and you begin to imagine the preacher is trying to undermine you, steal the affections of your people until he steals "your" church. Little by little you find yourself identifying faults in the young associate. You're becoming less friendly toward him, less encouraging and more critical of him. When others speak of him you find fault. You begin to cut back on his responsibilities for no real reason other than the fact that you have the power to do it, until finally the young preacher leaves.

The kingdom reality is this. What God has for you is for you. No one can take anything away from you that God has given to you. You can give it away by being ungrateful, mediocre, or by succumbing to jealousy, but no one can take it. That doesn't mean they won't try; it just means they won't succeed. Suppose they can preach better, teach better, possess better skills in other areas of leadership. So what! You have what it takes for your divine assignment. If more were required, you would have been given more. "Do you." Be your best "you."

When Someone is Jealous of You

When you're the object of someone's jealousy, you're in a very dangerous position. You're in the crosshair of the "fiery darts of the wicked." Don't try to rationalize it or look for logic. There is none. If their jealousy of you goes unchecked, it will

only degrade. It isn't the same as being the object of an admirer's envy (Envy in the Safe Zone). Be very clear about this. Jealousy is a murderer. Jealousy would claim self-defense but that plea would never stand the scrutiny of the Holy Spirit. Jealousy commits premeditated murder; spiritual murder in the 1st degree. The one guilty of murder by jealousy is guilty of the included lesser charges: anger, malicious envy, hatred, meanness, plotting, as well. It's most formidable weapon is the tongue; with the tongue, it can take you out. Jealousy will try to hurt you, demean you, embarrass you, discourage you, exclude you, eliminate you, destroy your reputation, undermine your work. Jealousy will do anything that will take you out of its equation.

Murder by Jealousy

[Spiritual]

1st Degree Murder

A person's jealousy toward you is not your fault. The problem lies within that person. You, however, as the object of another's jealousy, do have a threefold responsibility. (1) Compassion wants you to understand a jealous person isn't a bad person, but they are an insecure person. The seed of their insecurities were planted long before you ever came on the scene. Don't take it too personally. You're just a convenient target. There were others before you and there will be others after you. They would be jealous of almost anyone. Think of how it must feel to have an emotion that rises up within and gets out of hand. Jealousy doesn't travel alone; it's companions are envy, anger, spite, hatred, just to name a few. For a colleague to be jealous of another, it can't be a good feeling. No one enjoys being out of control. Being ruled by any emotion can't be a pleasant experience. In the midnight hour, in those dark quiet moments when no one else is around, even if but for a moment, the jealous person is not proud but rather ashamed of their feelings. That's not to say it's okay. It's just reminder that compassion has a voice in this matter.

Secondly, your responsibility is to protect yourself and your purpose. Within the context of this concern you can't make someone not be jealous but you can guard yourself if or when you find that you're the object of their jealousy. Of course, you cover the matter in prayer. It's bigger than you are. Jealousy has far too many warrior companions for you to deal with alone. Be smart and keep a safe distance from a jealous person. You can't fix jealousy. You can't love jealousy away, or love someone out of their jealousy. Step back! This demon is for the Holy Ghost alone.

Thirdly, keep watch on your "humility meter." Make sure you aren't doing anything to kindle the flame of jealousy in another person. Watch your mouth to make sure you aren't bragging in any way. Make sure your verbal praise and thanksgiving isn't a veneer for bragging. Humility says, "Whatever good is in me, I'm grateful to God for it and for the privilege of using it to God's glory." Paul says it's God who has begun the good work in you and it's God who performs it through you. Keep your head on straight.

Finally, this closing thought about jealousy. Jealousy is, above all things, an extreme lack of faith in God. It speaks loudly in one's spirit saying:

- God has given you less than someone else
- Someone else is better
- What God has given is insufficient
- God will allow someone to take what you have.

Jealousy doesn't see the big picture; the purpose God for bringing people into each other's lives. Jealousy is insecure and selfish, thinking only of itself and what it stands to lose.

C.L. Lawrence

PRAYERFULLY PONDER

1. Are you jealous of someone today? If so, why? Be honest.

_____

_____

_____

_____

2. What does a jealous spirit say about one's perception of God?

_____

_____

_____

_____

3. Note three scriptures that address the matter of jealousy.

_____

_____

_____

_____

ENVY & JEALOUSY	
ENVY 2 Entities At least 2 people	**JEALOUSY** 3 Entities 2+ people & 1 object of desire
You Want Something Someone Else Has	**Afraid Someone Is Going To Take What You Have**
Doesn't always carry a negative connotation	Always implies a feeling of resentment toward another.
Can be used to show a desire to equal another in achievement or excellence as in emulation. Desire to emulate doesn't have negative connotations.	Always negative
A reaction to lacking something	A reaction to the threat of losing something (church; notoriety)
The emotion when you want a position or notoriety that someone else has	The emotion when you fear you may be replaced in the affection of the people you love
To bear a grudge toward someone due to coveting what that person has or enjoys	Apprehensive or vengeful out of fear of being replaced by someone else.
In a milder sense: the longing for something someone else has without any ill will intended toward that person	It can also mean watchful, or anxiously suspicious.
When one lacks a desired attribute of another person.	When something we already have is threatened by another.

C.L. Lawrence

"Speak only if it improves upon the silence."

— Mahatma Gandhi

THE 6ᵀᴴ COMMANDMENT

THOU SHALL NOT KILL

THOU SHALL NOT KILL, IS A MORAL imperative included as one of the Ten Commandments in the Torah.ⁱⁱ The imperative to not kill is in the context of unlawful killing resulting in bloodguilt. The Hebrew Bible has many prohibitions against unlawful killing, but also has strict laws for lawful killing in the context of war, capital punishment, and self-defense. What's being discussed in the context of this commandment isn't about physically drawing blood, but it is about life and death. It is about the power of words to commit spiritual murder.

Some preachers say they ran from the call for a myriad of reasons. Well, just a cursory reading of Luke 6:45 alone is enough to make a thinking person run for the hills. That words reveal what's in the heart is simply reason enough to make anyone want to keep their mouth shut, much less desire to preach. A shower every day, maybe even twice a day, deodorant, tooth paste and mouth wash, all designed to cleanse the body at the start of the day so that it won't be offensive. But, who thinks of cleansing the heart so that their words won't be offensive.

ⁱⁱ Exodus 20:13 and Deuteronomy 5:17

In the old days if you were caught saying bad words, the teacher or your mom would wash your mouth out with soap. YUCK! While cussing, profanity, the use of those four-letter words is unbecoming and beneath the dignity of people of a holy nation,[jj] this commandment is concerned with something far more damaging, far more lethal than "bad words." It's concerned with the power in the choice and use of words. When we read the word "tongue" we know the Bible is referring to words. Death and life are in the power of the spoken word.[kk] There is death and life in the tongue or in words. Words can be used in ways that heal encourage and motivate others to fulfill their greatest potential, and bring leaders of nations to find common ground. Without the use of a single cuss word, words can be used to cause doubt and despair, start wars, and destroy the bonds that hold relationships together. There are no cleaning products, from mouthwash to industrial strength grease solvents able to cleanse dirty words or their effects once they're spoken. The best oral hygiene is powerless to sanitize words as they come out of the mouth because words come from the heart.

Have you checked what's in your heart lately, or ever? Please, don't be offended by the question. Think of the heart as a reservoir or storehouse. As a reservoir, are you pouring in fresh water daily, keeping the water moving. Is your heart a channel where living waters flow? John says, *"He who believes in Me, as the Scripture has said, out of his heart will flow rivers of living water."*[ll] As a storehouse, are you storing the Word daily, fresh food that will nourish, strengthen, and give hope, or are you storing stinky garbage, like undisciplined judgmental thought processes, anger, painful memories. Take a look at your Ego Meter;[mm] check yourself for the EGW virus.[nn] Daily spiritual cleansing, cleansing

---

[jj] I Peter 2:9

[kk] Proverb 18:21

[ll] John 7:38 (NKJV)

[mm] Ego Meter, See 1st Commandment

[nn] EGW: Ego Gone Wild, See 1st Commandment

of the heart is as important as daily physical cleansing. *For of the abundance of the heart the mouth speaks.*

This is so critically important. The fact is, you can't smell your own breath. Other people know your breath is offensive but you don't. You figure it out from their reactions. Once you do, you take steps to address it, right? *The heart is the reservoir from which the tongue draws it's speech* Take time to notice how people react to your communication. The old people used to say, "You can't smell yourself right away. By the time you smell yourself, you've been stinking for three days." Truth or old wise saying, who knows? Most would never dream of not bathing for three days, although there are those who seem to put it to the test. Unarguably, they've become accustomed to their own body odor. Likewise, you may not be able to hear your own voice. Take time to look around. You might find your words have left a trail of wounded and dead bodies on the side of the road behind and around you.

Teaching about the tongue gets a lot of print space in the scripture because God wants his proclaimers to understand the power you have in speech, the power of words. Between Genesis 1:3-30 (KJV), God talks a lot. Nine times it's written, "God said," speaking things into existence. He talked a lot in those 27 verses, using words to bring things into existence, giving directives concerning how each entity was to function. What's so incredible about the power of God's words just in the creation alone is that all remains in operation as spoken from the beginning.

In John 1, Jesus is called the Word that was present in the beginning, and now made flesh. The Word was crucified but the Word was also resurrected, and with power. Metaphorically, can you see the association of power and word?

83

Taking the high road, calling them *well-meaning,* but overzealous, believers spew hate on other believers over issues of biblical doctrine; matters not germane to the basic tenants of the faith such as mode of baptism, worship style, who gets to come to the Table and when…. Some lemon juice anointed, self-appointed, "kingdom meanies" use the Word of God as a sword[oo] against other believers. Their speech is devoid of grace notes,[pp] words that are exhorting, encouraging, uplifting, or edifying. This is simply a reflection of what's in their heart. Is this you?

If you don't control your tongue away from the pulpit, you won't be able to control it in the pulpit

Ephesians 4:29 gives a quite vivid description of what words can do, especially insulting slurs and words spoken in anger. Words have meaning and they can be spoken too quickly. They can be like a sword thrust into the heart of the hearers, bringing irreparable harm to the one to whom they're spoken. Proverbs 13:3 teaches "Whoever guards his mouth preserves his life; he who opens wide his lips come to ruin."

On Sermon Delivery

The primary mode of sermon delivery is audible voice, the spoken word. Though a sermon can be written for others to read, the call to preach demands that the sermon be preached. How ironic it is that the very thing upon which verbal communication depends, the thing that has the power to channel living waters and/or death dealing cruelties, is the very thing needed to deliver the Word of God. To further add to the curiosity of the irony is the relationship of the heart with the tongue. The heart is the reservoir from which the tongue draws its speech. The tongue directs traffic at the intersection of Grace

---

[oo] Hebrews 4:12
[pp] Words that reflect the melody of the fruit of the spirit

and Judgment; Condemnation and Justification; Life and Death. Think about that. The words you speak determine what the hearer perceives about God and receives from God. How sobering the thought that God allows the instrument of such power to lie within the sphere of human control. How alarming the thought that the cleansing of the heart lies within the power of decision to do or not to do "due diligence," not only as a requisite part of sermon preparation but necessary to one's total well-being. The call to preach is a call to watch your mouth. Ah, but, absent the power of the Holy Spirit, to not submit the tongue to the control of the Holy Spirit is a guaranteed danger. Pray the words of David, "Set a watch, O Lord, before my mouth; keep the doors of my lips."[qq] Get this right, Beloved, because if you don't (can't) control your tongue away from the pulpit, you won't be able to control it in the pulpit.

The Sacred Desk or Bully Pulpit

Wooden, glass, plexi-glass, modest, elaborate, traditional, contemporary; situated on the right, the left, in between, the elevated crow's nest, or on the floor, the pulpit is the place from which God speaks through the servants he's called. Some refer to the pulpit area as hallowed ground and the pulpit itself, the Sacred Desk. Whatever you choose to call it, traditionally, the pulpit and the pulpit area are, at the very least, God's space, symbolically the place from which God speaks.

There's nothing holy about the wood or any of the materials with which the pulpit is constructed. It's the symbolism ascribed to it by the church that makes it what it is. Symbolism is important as it offers touch points to cultural and faith traditions. Symbolism has voice. It speaks historically of every aspect of a culture. To honor and respect the symbolism of the pulpit space expresses reverence to who and what it

---

[qq] Psalm 141:3

represents. The degree to which we honor the pulpit space reflects the degree to which God is honored. Conversely, the degree to which one reverences God is reflected in the degree of respect given to the space from which the church has set apart for God to speak. In other words, how you see the pulpit determines your attitude and approach to it, and the message you deliver from it. If you see the pulpit as a stage, or an elevated platform upon which "you" are the focus, then your messages will reveal the arrogance of your spirit. If you view the pulpit as the place from which God speaks, then your attitude and your messages will reflect the very heart of God.

The Word of God is the authority; therefore, the pulpit area is the space representing God's authority, the space from which divine authority speaks forth. Humans are visual creatures. As the preacher stands in the pulpit space, right or wrong, all that the pulpit represents is transferred onto the preacher to a lesser or greater degree. Whatever the preacher brings, attitudes, ideologies, decorum, etc. sets the tone for reverence, or the lack thereof. Everything from words to image from the pulpit speaks forth as authoritative.

Who stands in the pulpit, of course, matters, however, our interest in this discussion isn't around the various requirements that give one the title and privilege of preaching from the Sacred Desk. The concern of this commandment is the integrity of the preaching moment wherein the use of words emanating from the mouth of the preacher is important. Preaching has changed through the centuries regarding personal style and delivery, hermeneutics, and homiletics. Regardless of what has changed over the centuries, the Good News of Jesus Christ and the centrality of the cross must never change. Herein is the essence of our concern. Simply this, what comes out of the preacher's mouth and from whence it comes. The Bible says, what's in your heart comes out in your speech. So, the preacher must have frequent and regular spiritual cardiac monitoring to guard against the negative motivations taking root and coming out as mean spirited or self-centered rhetoric, or personal propaganda. Sidebar: To preach extemporaneously within the prepared sermon and remain on point is a particular skill uncommon and not easily developed unless you're a very focused thinker. The preacher who thinks in a very focused way can **extemporize** within their prepared sermon with points that complement the theme without taking the congregation on an unrelated detour never to return. Using the lectionary and sticking to your manuscript will help tremendously if you have the tendency to take emotional detours off the main highway and cause accidents along the way. It, also, guards against "soapbox sermons," pontificating on your pet issues and grievances.

There's a certain awe, as it should be, about the pulpit. The man or woman of God, called, anointed, prepared, steps up to the Sacred Desk at that eagerly awaited moment, the moment when the congregation will hear from Heaven. It's God's moment. It's God's hour. Step up, but step aside. Let him have it. God has a right to unobstructed access to the hearts and minds of his people, and the people have a right to their God without the preacher in the way. Don't get irreverently comfortable in God's space. It isn't your bully pulpit, your personal space to advance your own agenda, or send out personal messages. You're called to share a life-giving Word, not to use the Word to chastise the people of God (beat the sheep), manipulate the feelings of the congregation, tell them off or get them straight with death dealing dogmatism that kill the sheep then blame them for dying. That's spiritual terrorism, a Kingdom felony for which mean spirited preachers have been guilty for years.

Ask yourself these questions: "How do I see a congregation? Who are they? What is my role in their lives?" There must be a level of respect for the congregation as the people of God, and individuals as likenesses of yourself. You are no better than they, no worse than they, but equals in the sight of God, on a journey in which your call is to speak life-giving messages from the Word of God and lead the people home.   Philippians 2:3 (Amplified Bible) Do nothing from selfishness or empty conceit [through factional motives, or strife], but with [an attitude of] humility [being neither arrogant nor self-righteous], regard others as more important than yourselves.

Have respect for their time and their choice to be under the sound of your voice and not another. Though they love you, the congregation didn't come to hear about your problems or a steady diet of your personal feelings.   They have problems of their own. They're coming

> Your call is to speak life-giving messages from the Word of God to lead the people safely home

with the hope that you, the called one, will speak a word of hope that they can hold on to. They come hoping you can put them in touch with Jesus, or at the very least, bring their problems and issues to God's attention.   They come hoping that their weak faith will be strengthened by something God will say through you. Hoping you will help them find their way to Jesus, the healer, the deliverer, the provider, the forgiver; the one who is the father of mercy and God of all comfort;[rr] the one who's mercies are new every morning.[ss]   The preacher may be broken but the pulpit isn't the place for the breakdown. It's the place to call for the breakthrough. "If the leader can't handle life's struggles, what hope is there for me." The pulpit isn't your vertical sofa for a personal cathartic experience. It's there for the people of God to hear from God.

Life isn't something you can control.   Storms rage, sickness or grief may catch us by surprise, mistakes, disappointments, betrayal, … You can be thrown off your game at any time, in many ways, for various reasons. Life happens. Say it with me. Life happens. It happens to everyone. No one

[rr] II Corinthians 1:3
[ss] Lamentations 3:22-23

is exempt. No one gets through this life without struggle, without some pain and disappointment, not even the preacher. The preacher is human, therefore subject to all the struggles and fluctuations of life as is any other human being. Yet, while you can't control life, you can control how you navigate through it.

Lean & Preach

The preacher is called to a very tough task; to bring feelings, attitudes, and emotions under control so that the preacher isn't preaching personal situations and opinions, or speaking from a place of unresolved hurts and struggles. The preacher is called to step away from him or herself and be a vessel, an instrument of God's grace that God uses in the moment, no matter what personal challenges they're facing. The call to preach is the call to discipline; to set self aside and allow God to have the moment. If God is permitted to speak so much happens in the spirit realm at preaching time. As the word goes forth, power goes forth and falls where it's needed, even on the preacher. Don't take lightly the need for keen awareness on this point because the healthiest ego can become weak in the moment. No matter what you're going through, you're called to serve the Word. Always leaning on the Holy Spirit, there will be times when you're particularly weak and must lean more heavily. Lean and preach.

WATCH YOUR MOUTH
SPEAK LIFE • SPEAK HEALING

Prayer: *Dear Lord, Let the words of my mouth and the meditation of my heart be acceptable in your sight, O Lord, my rock and my redeemer. (Ps. 19:14); set a guard, O Lord, over my mouth; keep watch over the door of my lips! (Ps.141:3)*

1. Death and life are in the power of the tongue, and those who love it will eat its fruits. Proverbs 18:21

2. Let no corrupting talk come out of your mouths, but only such as is good for building up, as fits the occasion, that it may give grace to those who hear. Ephesians 4:29

3. But what comes out of the mouth proceeds from the heart, and this defiles a person. Matthew 15:18

4. There is one whose rash words are like sword thrusts, but the tongue of the wise brings healing. Proverbs 12:18

5. A word fitly spoken is like apples of gold in a setting of silver. Proverbs 25:11

6. Whoever guards his mouth preserves his life Proverbs 13:3a

7. A gentle tongue is a tree of life, but perverseness in it breaks the spirit. Proverbs 15:4

8. Let your speech always be gracious, seasoned with salt, so that you may know how you ought to answer each person. Colossians 4:6

9. Pleasant words [are as] an honeycomb, sweet to the soul, and health to the bones. Proverbs 16:24

10. Your word is a lamp to my feet and a light to my path. Psalm 119:105

Notes

"For I bear them record that they have a zeal for God, but not according to knowledge.

Romans 10:2

THE 7TH COMMANDMENT

THOU SHALL DO THY HOMEWORK

To a child probably the most distasteful thing about school was homework. It gets in the way of after school plans, TV time, game time, chillin' and "my time." If you were a good student, you couldn't sit down and quickly put something together just to get it done. It took time, thought, and reflection. You couldn't rush through it because it would be graded or evaluated in some way. Your grasp of the subject matter and your academic performance was a reflection of the level of work you put into your homework. And, Oh! By the way, not doing homework was not an option.

Echoing throughout time is the crescendo of children's voices asking the question, "Why do we have to do homework? Then children grow up only to find out that the dreaded personal time robber is still alive and following you everywhere you go and in everything you do. Homework is just simply an integral part of living out your best in life. It's where personal growth, learning and success begin and is cultivated. For the preacher, it's where the power begins. It's where the Holy Spirit meets you and much like the teacher checking your assignment and giving you a grade, the Holy Spirit pours out the anointing and power in direct correlation with your commitment to the homework.

The persons like in the Romans 10:2 text are important to remember. These are they, immature in their call, perceiving preaching as an event with only the pulpit, microphone and congregation in view. Many answer the call to preach the Good News of Jesus Christ with the best intentions but clueless as to the intricacies of the call. Still others wrestle with the call before surrendering, and rightly so, as they recognize preaching to be more than the charismatic delivery of a message to a captive audience. The responsibilities inherent in the call begin before and transcend the manuscript and the mic

There are gifted, articulate, charismatic orators, great speakers who write great speeches that move crowds to action, whose giftedness in that area surpasses the best preachers of the day; but oratorical skills and writing ability do not a preacher make. What sets the preacher aside from the enabled aforementioned is the divine call of God and the anointing of the Holy Spirit on the life of the preacher to be an instrument of God's amazing Grace, to deliver truths and principles that do more than move a crowd, but breathes life-giving messages, awakens the spirit, changes hearts and transforms the minds of people in the crowd.

Despite what you've observed in the preaching ministry of others, or what you've heard or imagined, there's more than what you see. Just as Jesus said to his disciples in John 16:12 that he had more to reveal to them, more than they could bear at the time, so the Holy Spirit will reveal that which is hidden. Consider the timeless principles of God like treasure hidden in a field. The Holy Spirit will peel back the layers of mystery and reveal the hidden treasures in the realm of the ministry of proclaiming the Good News as you faithfully do your homework along the way. Once you experience the beauty of what God shares, you will crave more. Homework is the excavation tool that will unearth "the more" that will satiate your spirit. Homework also gives you the full course meal to serve to God's people; nourishment they need but will never get it for themselves.

Three Categories of Preachers

There are three brands or categories of preachers in the Kingdom of God, "The Excavator," "The Jackleg,." and "The Milkman."

1. The Excavator

An excavator is a person who digs in a particular and controlled manner. Consider excavators of archeological digs, of ancient ruins, and prehistoric sites. They methodically and meticulously dig for artifacts, inscriptions, monuments, and other such remains for analysis and study of historic or prehistoric peoples and their culture. He/she goes to the dig knowing what they're looking for but open to the possibilities of finding the wonderfully unexpected. Not every person skilled to dig is qualified to be an excavator. There's a mindset that puts one in the category of excavator. The excavator while knowing his/her skill is humbled to be included among the few invited or chosen for the dig. They recognize the privilege of being included in the company of his/her peers. They've made the necessary sacrifice and lifestyle adjustments and rid themselves of superficial baggage so that nothing hinders the activity of the dig. The excavator preacher sees the field of study as filled with the possibility of discovering priceless treasures from the Word of God.

2. The Jackleg

There are few things in the universe worse than a "jackleg" preacher. A preacher who stands before the waiting congregation held captive by good church manners, suffering the reverberations of a sounding brass and tinkling cymbal as Rev. Jackleg, having not properly done his/her homework causes their ears to bleed. Harsh words, indeed. What sets the jackleg apart from the Excavator, aside from having an unteachable spirit and an EGW[tt] (Ego Gone Wild)? Simply this, the Excavator honors and completes the homework assignments and the Jackleg does not. The jackleg approaches the mic ill-prepared and isn't above presenting stolen sermons.[uu] The jackleg doesn't consider the needs of the congregation, but instead what he/she needs from the congregation: accolades, affirmation, a good offering or honorarium. A polished jackleg is like a con man. He/she can get away with it for a while but the gift of discernment is present in every gathering of God's people. Someone sees through the jackleg and spots the absence of the true anointing from the beginning. Others don't. Eventually, however, the jackleg is revealed. Don't be a jackleg preacher.

3. The Milkman

In the old days milk was delivered to your door by the milkman. You knew him and he knew you. He didn't bring meat and you didn't expect that of him. He was faithful. You could depend on him to bring the milk. As you opened your door, you knew exactly what you were expecting and how much you were getting. He picked up the milk from the same place, took the same route, and delivered it at the same time to the same customers. If you wanted two bottles, you got two. If you wanted four bottles, you got four. Nothing more, nothing less. If you didn't ask for more, you didn't get more. You never had to worry about what was coming. It was milk. It had little variety; skim milk, 2% fat, no-fat, chocolate milk, but that was about it. Just milk. It always came from the same source so the

---

[tt] EGW Ego Gone Wild. See "Ego Gone Wild," See in 1st Commandment
[uu] A stolen sermon is one taken from another preacher or the internet and re-preached word for word

quality was not in question. All you had to do was receive it; nothing to think about, just open the door and take the milk in.[vv]

That perfectly describes the preacher who doesn't hone his/her craft, explore new ideas to incorporate, or expand their knowledge base to include more of the Word. They show up time after time the same way with the same thing. Of course, you'll always have milk in your delivery vehicle but don't let that be all there is.

Reflect a few seconds about the milkman who delivered milk to your door. Time changes everything. In the 21st century, milk delivery by the milkman alone is obsolete. People go to the market and choose among a variety of milks, different brands, flavors, textures, origins. Choices. It's no longer just plain old cow's milk anymore. Even more progressive is shopping online. Shoppers order what they want (milk, meat, etc.) and an unknown person delivers. The delivery person doesn't know or care about the shopper and the shopper doesn't care about the delivery person. Sounds a lot like TV church, doesn't it?

The point is this. The job as a milkman is an entry level position, a rooky level job. Start there but don't stay there because you'll soon become unnecessary. While people will always need milk, they'll shop in ways and places where they can get the milk and more.

Homework

Think of the call to ministry as having two parts. Part I, the call to prepare for service and Part II, the execution of the call, in whatever capacity that service may be. Given that the sermon begins long before the preacher approaches the sacred desk, let's begin by just scratching the surface of the

---

[vv] I Peter 2:2 As newborn babes, desire the sincere milk of the word, that ye may grow thereby:

"Homework" inherent in the call. If you're to be an effective proclaimer of the Good News of Jesus Christ, a prepared instrument of the Grace of God in the hands of a mighty God, you must do your homework and understand that the assignments are perpetual. None of the assignments are easy but each one is of indispensable value.

Assignment #1

Look Down at Your Feet

Maybe you preach in a cultural tradition where the people "talk back" and they seem to always "get with you." Look down at your feet. Maybe the "Amen Corner" is loud and clear and doesn't miss a beat. Look down at your feet. Maybe you preach in a worship tradition where the congregation is quiet during the sermon but they applaud at the end and the applause for you is always enthusiastic. Look down at your feet. Maybe you preach like Peter did on Pentecost and 3,000 come to Christ every time you preach. Look down at your feet. Maybe at the end of the worship experience you can't get to your office or to your car because the people are shaking your hand, hugging you and telling you how great your sermon was. Look down at your feet.

It doesn't matter how many sermons you've preached and set the congregation ablaze. Look down at your feet. It doesn't matter how many preaching engagements you've had to turn down because you're booked out for the next seven years. Look down at your feet. Why on earth would you look down at your feet? What are you looking for? You're looking down to be sure your feet are on the ground.

It's easy to get swept away by the reaction of the people. It's human nature to want to feel good about what you do. Everyone wants and needs affirmation especially the preacher when his/her purpose in the call is to give, to be an instrument of God's amazing Grace, to be a channel through whom the

Holy Spirit can flow. The line is very fine between your feet on the ground and walking on air. It's remembering that it's the Word of God you're preaching; that the power is his power given to you by the Holy Spirit. God's trusting you to give him the glory and not take it for yourself, not even for a moment. As important as the sermon is, equally, if not more important is the spiritual condition of the vessel through whom the sermon is delivered. The best sermon on paper or your iPad is powerless if the preacher is in the way, grandstanding.

Consistently and routinely look down at your feet. It's important to be honest with yourself about yourself. No one knows you better than you know yourself. You know your level of neediness and it's wise to do a self-assessment from time to time. Do you need lots of accolades? When you don't get it, you feel defeated? Do you seek admiration? When you don't get enough, do you feel insecure? Do you need to be reminded of how good you are? When you don't get the reminders, you get worried and wonder what's wrong. Having that mentor you prayed for in the 3rd Commandment is crucial to keeping you grounded. Your mentor is one person you can trust to tell you to look down at your feet because you've crossed the fine line and walking on air.

Assignment #2

Know the Congregation

This is a pitfall that many preachers fall into; not just rooky preachers but seasoned preachers as well, not knowing the congregation. If you're a pastor of a small to mid-size congregation and you've been in position for a while, don't dismiss this assignment or take it for granted. Unlike in the old days when you could reach a level of familiarity and comfort with the families and members in your community and congregational growth was static, congregations are ever changing. Two and three car families give family members the option of going outside of the community to other churches; likewise, visitors come and go. Visitors, even just one, by their mere presence alter the tone in the sanctuary; change the dynamic and the mood of the congregation for that Sunday. They're a guest of someone and the host is happy the visitor is there. Maybe they're a stranger; now everyone is aware of their presence.

This is not to suggest your sermon should change because visitors are present. It is to suggest that you take the time to be aware of who's sitting in the pews. Homogeneous groups are no longer the norm, and a homogeneous group doesn't mean the same thoughts and passions exist for the whole group. Perhaps it never did.

The world is changing faster than ever. Cyberspace, the internet, the information super highway, and social networks have exposed the once sheltered community to a world of different ideologies, opening minds, increasing tolerance, raising awareness of many issues, inviting questions, doubt and debate. This isn't necessarily a bad thing because thinking is never a bad thing. Because of access and exposure to the world congregations change and fluctuate in their thinking from week to week. To some degree you have a different congregation every week.

Often the media sets the agenda for thought and conversation, moves the direction of discourse, and influences opinions. People are bombarded with sound bites about terrorism, global warming, politics, social issues, the economy, gun control, police shootings, world hunger, who's in the closet, who's coming out of the closet, is the closet door open or closed, same sex marriage, on and on. Your assignment is to know the congregation so that you can preach a fresh, right now Word in a relevant context, not a sermon that hit a home run forty-seven years ago. Rotating sermons doesn't work. Yes, the Word is timeless, and truth is eternal, but things change within eternity. Don't be lazy, kicking your feet up and resting on "there's nothing new under the sun." Though there is nothing new under the son, there's a lot new to you. Do your homework. If you can't write new sermons, the least you can do is remix the old ones and make them new.

Assignment #3

Pulpit Etiquette

While the call to ministry is a call to service, it's a high level of service at a professional level. Therefore, see yourself as a professional and handle yourself as such. Walk in the dignity of the call. If you expect respect for the call, then you must handle yourself in such a way that your respect for the call, who you are and what you do is without question. Ultimately you must set the tone and standard of dignity for yourself and for your work.

As you interact in different places in the body of Christ, professional protocol isn't always in place. Where protocol isn't evident you must operate in your own professional etiquette. Laity and even other preachers will tell you it isn't important. Set a standard for yourself and never give place to mediocrity. Good manners and professionalism will always cause you to stand out. God can move you to the next level when he sees that you know how to handle yourself beyond where you are in the present.

Invitation to Preach

When you receive an invitation from anyone other than the pastor of the church, take the time to do things correctly. Laity is very likely unaware of professional etiquette, neither should they be expected to know, but you must. People say, this is our church and this is how we do things. Nevertheless, while you're not there to change the culture of the church, you are always to maintain the dignity of the office of the preaching ministry.

Always be certain the person extending the invitation has the authority to do so? Have they gone through the proper protocol to extend the invitation? Asking for clarification is wise and simply good manners. Asking the simple question, "Do you have your pastor's approval to extend this invitation? Or, "Has the pastor approved me as the choice for this engagement? Never take for granted that proper protocol has been followed. Take responsibility for all the dynamics concerning your ministry. To do so will avoid embarrassing moments for yourself and others. At some point before the engagement, check off the following items:

1. Speak to the pastor personally as a gesture of respect
2. Time you're expected to arrive
3. Does the pastor prefer you to wear a robe?
4. Do you join the congregation in the worship experience from the Call to Worship or do you remain in the pastor's study until someone comes for you? This varies denominationally and culturally.
5. Do you extend the call to discipleship or does the pastor do that?

Do your homework on the congregation. Don't just come preaching, presuming to do so from your comfort zone. Ask the questions that will give the relevant context to your content.

1. What is the average age in the congregation, percentage of youth and seniors, cultural diversity, if any? You need to know such information because you want to be careful about using language, colloquialisms, clichés, and idioms that the congregation may or may not understand.

2. What length sermon is the congregation accustomed to? Congregations find sermons that are too short equally distasteful as sermons that are too long.

3. Have there been any recent tragedies in the congregation or community which may be affecting them (police shootings, natural disaster, celebrations, etc.)? You may not want to build your sermon around the event but compassion demands that you acknowledge it.)

Do your homework on "Who's Who." Ignore this and you may never preach there again. Seemingly small things, little oversights offend people so you have to watch out for that. Find out the names and briefly and respectfully acknowledge each one:

- Pastor's spouse (if there is one)
- Denominational dignitaries (If applicable)
- Chairpersons of the event
- Chairpersons of the key leadership organizations. This will vary in different denominations (deacons, stewards, trustees, etc.)

Assignment #4

Show Honor & Respect to Authority

Calling your attention to this may seem unnecessary and unimportant contingent upon the manners and customs of your faith tradition. Expressions of honor, respect and good manners will always serve you well. Cover your bases because laity can't be expected to think on the level of clergy. When you speak to the pastor prior to the engagement you'll cover these items so on the day of the engagement it should not be an issue.

Scenario #1: You're being invited into the Pastor's office in his/her absence

Never go into a Pastor's office in their absence. Respectfully decline the invitation to do so. Ladies, if you need to change clothing, ask for an alternative place. Some pastors really don't mind if you go into their office, others do.

Scenario #2: You're being invited into the pulpit before the pastor arrives

Don't do it. Wait for the pastor unless you know in advance or he/she has sent word that they'll be late or absent. Otherwise, just don't do it. Better to ere on the side of caution. If everything has been put in order and it's okay to enter the pulpit in the pastor's absence, don't sit in the pastor's seat if you know he/she's coming. Wait until they arrive and extend the invitation to you to sit in the center seat. It's the pastor's privilege to offer you their seat. The Bible tells us it's better to take the seat of lower estate and be invited up, rather than to take the seat of high esteem and be told to come down.[ww]

- Don't go into the pulpit before the pastor
- Don't sit in the center seat until you've been invited to do so

Be a Class Act

This is completely optional. No one will tell you this. If you don't do it, no one will call you on it. Send a thank you note to the pastor. Even if your friend was the one who submitted your name for the engagement, it was subject to the pastor's approval so acknowledge that with a note of appreciation. In a thank you note, consider returning a tithe of the offering to the church that invited you. You can either send the tithe to the organization which invited you or to the pastor saying he/she

[ww] Luke 14:8-11

can use it for the church's project or initiative of his/her choice. This isn't in any rule book for preachers. It's just a gesture of humility, honor, and good manners. Be a class act. Set a standard. God will help you with your dreams if you help others with theirs.

PRAYERFULLY PONDER

Answer the following questions honestly. No one will see your answers except you and God.

1. Which category of preacher do you fall into, The Excavator, The Jackleg, or The Milkman? Why?

_____

_____

_____

_____

_____

	Yes	No
2. Do you need lots of accolades?	___	___
3. When you don't get it, do you feel defeated?	___	___
4. Do you seek admiration?	___	___
5. When you don't get enough, you feel insecure?	___	___
6. Do you need to be reminded of how good you are?	___	___
7. When you don't get the reminders, you get worried and wonder what's wrong?	___	___

If you answered Yes to any of the above questions, please prayerfully review the 1st Commandment.

	Invitation to Preach Pulpit Etiquette Check List	✓
1	Re-read the Homework section	
2	Know the Congregation: Average age, % of youth vs. seniors; traditional; contemporary; cultural diversity, …	
3	**Do Not** Preach on controversial issues (No politics, No sex, No Same Sex issues, …)	
4	Speak to the pastor upon receiving the invitation if it didn't come from him/her	
5	Time you're expected to arrive	
6	Does the pastor prefer you to wear a robe?	
7	Do you join the congregation in the worship experience from the Call to Worship or do you remain in the pastor's study until someone comes for you? This varies denominationally and culturally.	
8	Do you extend the call to discipleship or does the pastor do that?	
9	What length sermon is the congregation accustomed to?	
10	"Who's Who" (for proper acknowledgements)	

C.L. Lawrence

THE 8TH COMMANDMENT

THOU SHALL NOT STEAL

C AN YOU WALK INTO A HOSPITAL NURSERY, pick up a baby you like when no one is looking, take that baby, show it to people and say it's your baby? Yes, you can do that but that doesn't make it your baby. That baby, as beautiful and precious as it is, has nothing of you; not your features, blood type, DNA, nothing. You see the baby is beautiful but you don't know any more about the baby than that. You know nothing of the baby's origin or health record. You only know that the baby is beautiful, you took it and called it your own. Guess what? Someone knows you were never pregnant. Shame on you!

Can you go to the bakery, get the best cake in the showcase, bring it home, put it on the table and tell the family or guests that you baked it? Of course, you can. Only you and perhaps those who know you can't bake would know you didn't bake it. You can get away with it for a while until someone asks for your recipe or asks something as simple as where you shop for the ingredients or how long you let it cool before putting it on the cake plate. Now you've got to start lying. Guess what? Someone can tell the difference between a store-bought cake and a homemade cake. Shame on you! To have that awesome homemade cake you must follow the recipe to the letter; put in the right ingredients in the right sequence, put it in the oven and wait for it to bake.

For a woman to give birth to her own biological child she must go through the normal stages of the gestation period; stages common to every pregnancy. There are lifestyle disciplines she must adopt to create the best environment for the baby to develop. It takes time. Then there's the period of labor. Though it may differ in time and intensity, there is struggle and work involved, hence, the term "labor."

When it comes to the sermon, go through the labor, and give birth to your own baby. Don't kidnap someone else's baby. It won't resemble you. Nothing of you will be reflected in a kidnapped baby. Perceptive and discerning people will know it isn't your baby. Get a cookbook or go somewhere and learn how to bake a cake. Don't buy it and claim you baked it. A homemade cake looks different and tastes different. Perceptive and discerning people will know if you baked it. Do your own work. Let the Lord use you. Allow the Lord to give you something to give to his people.

Do your own work

Preaching time is a moment in time, like a freeze frame moment in eternity. It's a sacred moment. It's that moment when God brings his selected people together in a specific time to speak to them. Remember, you do the work so that God can use you as a vessel which includes your personality, your voice, everything about you. You don't choose the audience so don't waste time thinking about who should be there to hear your message. Just make sure that it's "you" who's there.[xx] God's got everything under control. It isn't your message, it's God's message. The ones present are the ones who need to hear it.

[xx] 2nd Commandment: Thou Shall Be Thine Authentic Self

Preach a Fresh Word

Re-preaching another preacher's sermon word for word isn't preaching the sermon, it's regurgitating what someone else has preached or reciting someone else's manuscript. It isn't you. It isn't your voice. It isn't yours. Your sermon draws its breath in your spirit first; from the prayers you've prayed throughout the time you spent with it and the work done on it. Your sermon finds energy in points you've wrestled with, questions the scriptures have asked of you and you've asked of the scriptures. Its life comes from the passion of your soul and the soul of your passion. It feeds your soul before it reaches the ears of the people. When the sermon is yours, it ministers to your spirit. At times, you'll wrestle with what you're saying, interpreting it through the lens of your life experience, perhaps even argue with your interpretation, challenging yourself to think and not repeat. That's the process of it becoming your own.

Some preachers go online for the manuscripts or buy CDs of another preacher's sermon and they don't even bother to remix it. They just preach it word for word. That's not preaching. That's stealing. Don't do that. You can steal the words but you can't steal the anointing. Without the anointing, you don't have a sermon, you only have words with no power and no effect. You've not only stolen the sermon but you've abused the people, disrespected their time and trust. They may not know it but over time your emptiness will show. You'll be a sounding brass and a tinkling cymbal. Away from the mic you won't sound like the person at the mic. Every sermon has a signature. There's something of you in your every sermon. It reflects the author just as a child resembles and reflects the parent.

Every sermon has a signature

C.L. Lawrence

There will always be things in sermons that are impressive and speak to you personally. That's the fragrance from the oil. There's that line or principle that jumps out and you say, "I'm going to use that." Great! Use it! God's truth is out there in the public domain of the universe without a copyright. Use it but not word for word. When you do lift statements from another's work, quote. Give proper credit.

> Every time you steal a sermon,
> you're putting your name
> on the birth certificate of a baby
> that isn't yours.

Honor your colleague whether contemporary or historic. It's a matter of intellectual honesty and professional integrity. Give credit where credit is due. Honor your colleague or from whomever you got it with a proper acknowledgement. It's a matter of intellectual honesty. Represent God with integrity. There are preachers we love and admire, perhaps historical figures like Rev. Dr. Martin Luther King, Jr., Rev. Jarena Lee, or contemporaries like Bishop Millicent Hunter or Bishop TD Jakes. Glean from the anointing on their sermons but don't steal their sermons. You don't know what valley or struggle gave birth to their message, what fear or pain gave voice to their sermon and you wouldn't want to go through someone else's journey. Preach from your own journey, from your own joys and tears, from your own wounds and healings.

The notion of standing as a vessel through whom the very God of eternity will speak is a daunting thought. No one wants to flunk, fail, or come up empty. To think of yourself called to the great cloud of preaching witnesses such as the Apostle Paul, Charles Haden Spurgeon, Gardner Taylor, Billy Graham, George Buttrick, Jeremiah Wright, Prathia LauraAnn Hall, Vashti M. McKenzie, Carolyn Ann Knight, ... is enough

112

to make you question your own call. Paul answers the question this way in Philippians 1:6, "Being confident of this very thing, that he which hath begun a good work in you will perform it until the day of Jesus Christ." The work you're called to do is a work God has put in you and he will carry out the work.

Preach What You Know

Preach what you know. You can give directions to places you've already been; describe paintings you've seen and music you've heard. You can't show the way to where other preachers have been, describe paintings they've seen or music they've heard. Preach what YOU know. So much lies within your soul to teach and share and encourage. You know every crack and pothole in the road of your journey from brokenness to wholeness; every hill and dale on your way from hopelessness and despair to the blessed life. You know every nuance on the journey from fear to faith; and from worry to worship. You know what it is to go through the valley of the shadow of death and finally come out on the other side; to go through a storm and be cold and wet when it's over but still alive. You know that weeping may endure for a night and the night may last not hours but weeks, months, or years; but morning will come and with it comes joy. Preach what you know; that's why you know it. That's why God took you through it. Turn on your lamp with the Word God has given to you and let your light so shine to illuminate the pathway for others to see their way.

Preach what you know That's why you know it!

Manage Your Time

As a preacher, you're not a preacher only. You're a pastor, spouse, mother, father, grandparent, sibling, friend, neighbor, entrepreneur, employee, colleague, … You wear many hats, put out fires, voices clamoring as you try to respond to everyone who has a want. All these areas are important but if you don't set your priorities and manage your time, then the vicissitudes of life will steal your time and YIKES! It's sermon time again. There are hundreds of books written on time management. Choose anyone you like; the principles are essentially the same.

Yikes!

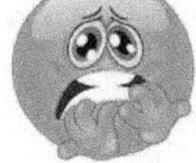

It's sermon time already!

Prioritize. Prioritize. Prioritize. The good news is that in Christ it's easier to prioritize. In the world, you have competition with which to consider and contend. With that element removed from your time equation in Christ, you'd be surprised how much more time and energy you have available to do your own work.

Stealing is a Crap Shoot

Last, but certainly not least. Stealing a sermon is a crap shoot, a roll of the dice. You're gambling no one in the congregation has heard it before, and they do listen. Consider this. The preacher is no longer the most educated or well-read individual in the congregation. If you've read it, so has someone else. Secondly, Christendom is a small world. People share CDs and downloads. With the advent of the internet, social media, YouTube, Face Book, and countless preaching networks on the world wide web, if you've seen or heard the preacher, you can bet someone in the congregation has also. Face it. If a sermon isn't memorable, who would steal it. If it is memorable, then it's probable that someone remembers it.

Excerpts are find. Quotes are fine. Just remember. Give credit where credit is due. Your integrity depends on it.

PRAYERFULLY PONDER

My Method of Time Management

Poor time management is the biggest thief of sermon preparation time. Describe your method or system of time management. If your system is good and works for you, then write it down and share it with a colleague. If you don't have a system, or your system needs improvement, this is the perfect time to make the necessary adjustments.

_____

_____

_____

_____

_____

_____

_____

_____

_____

_____

_____

_____

_____

_____

C.L. Lawrence

Therefore, since we are surrounded by such a huge crowd of witnesses to the life of faith, let us strip off every weight that slows us down, **especially the sin that so easily trips us up.** *And let us run with endurance the race God has set before us.*

Hebrews 12:1

THE 9TH COMMANDMENT

THOU SHALL KNOW THY DEMONS

(BECAUSE THEY KNOW YOU)

The goal of this commandment isn't to teach demonology, amuse or frighten you in any way. The purpose is, as with each commandment, to give you substantive thoughts to ponder; thoughts that will nudge you to walk circumspectly and steer you toward excellence on your journey in the ministry of preaching. This commandment, though the commentary is the shortest, is particularly important because in the busyness of life, juggling responsibilities, and giving the sincerest effort to honor the call to ministry, things can naturally be overlooked.

In the beginning, God

At the very moment you drew your first breath and those present laid their eyes on you marveling at what a beautiful baby you were, at that twinkling of time, your earthly life story began its chronicle on the pages of eternity. No one comes into the world as a blank slate, but that wonder filled moment at the birth of a new life does not disclose that this tiny little person already has a history. At birth, emerging from the womb was a manifestation of God's imagination. You were new to your mother and the rest of the human race but you were not new to the universe or, more specifically, you were known by God.

Paul speaks of your presence in the consciousness of God, being loved and chosen in Christ before the foundation of the world;[yy] predestined to be conformed to the image of Christ.[zz] You were there somewhere in eternity past and you were fully known by God. That's the spiritual reality. In the beginning, God ... from which you must mark your beginning, your history, your spiritual ancestry. Even if you don't know the names in between you must mark your beginning with God. David speaks of God's awareness and very intentional "hands on" as you were in your mother's womb,[aaa] so there was never a time that you weren't connected with God even before earthly life began. That's an awesome thought. Being with God in eternity past and down through the corridor of time to the moment of your birth proves the point made in the 2nd Commandment, you were not an OOPS!

Regardless of the circumstances of your conception, your birth was not a mistake and your life isn't a fluke. Your parents may or may not have planned you but be certain of this, God planned you and has plan for your life. He wasn't surprised at your conception or confused about what to do with you at your birth. He is able to work all things for his own good.

As briefly referenced in the 4th Commandment, contrary to The Tabula Rasa, [bbb] the blank slate theory of human development, we now know babies aren't born as blank slates on any level. Babies come into this world with volumes of code and genetic predispositions written on their DNA. At times, we're fortunate enough to see personality traits and exceptional gifts

---

[yy] Ephesians 1:4
[zz] Romans 8:29
[aaa] Psalm 139:13-16
[bbb] The Tabula Rasa (blank slate) theory of human development, credited to English philosopher, John Locke and Swiss philosopher Jean-Jacques Rousseau

passed from one generation to the next. Other times you look at a person and wonder where that particular gift or behavior came from. Often giving careful ear to the elders will reveal information or secrets that connect the dots. Whether apparent, it's all there somewhere.

So it is when you step up to answer the call to preach -- the birth of a new preacher. Enthusiastic, humbled and thankful, but never blank. There's volumes written on the DNA of your life history that you bring to the call. Whether you answer the call at 18 or 80 you don't step up to the call alone. Howbeit, visible or invisible, with you are the people and their impact on your life, their thoughts and interpretations that have passed down and either shaped or influenced your you in some way. You bring your past with you, the experiences of your childhood and beyond, your perceptions and your realities, the vestiges of your life. You bring interpretations of the world around you, trials and tribulations, successes and failures, ideologies, philosophies, superstitions, doubts, and fears. You bring every insult that hurt you, every affirmation that encouraged you, opinions and beliefs that find their authenticity not in the academy but oral history. All of it matters, the good, the bad, the ugly; everything matters because it all culminates into the authentic you. Every experience is like the stroke of a paint brush on the canvas of your life.

The Good

The Bad

The Ugly

Everything Matters

Who Else Was in the Delivery Room

At the birth of a child there are at least a few people present in the delivery room associated with the birth, each having a specific role; the medical professionals and whomever they allow to witness the birth, and, of course, the mom. This is the visible crowd, but in the spirit realm there are others present.

Paul speaks of the spiritual warfare wherein principalities, powers, rulers of darkness, and spiritual wickedness in high places,[ccc] referring to a highly organized military in the spirit realm that targets for attack the children of God. If you read too quickly you'll miss what's between the lines. In any warfare, there's strategy. The efficacy of the enemy's strategy or plan of attack is dependent upon the amount and quality of knowledge obtained about the target of attack. In other words, the more knowledge the enemy collects about you the better the chances of his victory over you.

What better strategy for the enemy to get to know you then to assign "spiritual stalkers" to meet you as soon as possible, at the moment of birth, stay with and watch you grow. They don't have to do or say anything to you, just take note of your proclivities, watch the habits and appetites you develop. Then at opportune times the enemy can introduce temptations based on the knowledge obtained by just watching and waiting. There's no guest work on the part of the enemy. He knows what will tempt you and what will not. Don't make the mistake in thinking there's good or bad luck involved or things just happen. That thought, too, is a trick of the enemy. He plays a well-designed game of strategy. He's been honing it since he was kicked out of heaven. He's good at it. Just like in football, he's studied your playbook and he's got his own.

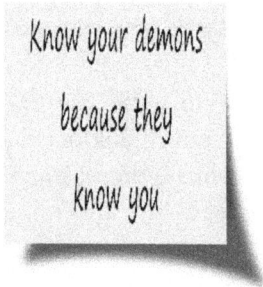

Know your demons because they know you

The battleground is the mind. Warfare takes place in the mind. The mind is receptive to subtle suggestions and the enemy knows that. Your mind is particularly receptive when you're tired, weary, lonely, sad, disappointed, feeling defeated, … The use of questions is a great way to get your mental attention.

[ccc] Ephesians 6:12

"Aren't you tired of being lonely?' "Don't you think if things were going to change they would have by now?" "You're stuck. What are you going to do?" With the seeds planted firmly in your mind, now the enemy can suggest solutions. Everyone's been there at one time or another. For the purposes of this short consideration, it's not about whether you took the bait. The question is, "Do you recognize the bait?" Know your demons because they know you.

Don't be Fooled by Bedtime Stories or Hollywood Images

The enemy and demons are portrayed as big ugly fire breathing dragons, or an ugly dude with horns, a red suit and a tail, or really ugly nasty monstrous looking rascals that run around hiding in closets and under the bed. Who in the world would listen long enough to be tempted or lured in by something like that. Neither are those images consistent with the description of Lucifer in scripture. [ddd] Nevertheless, the physical descriptions of demons aren't nearly as important as their alluring nature. Watch out for those darling little demons that suck you in. Watch out for those

demons that have become so familiar that you don't mind them being around. Watch out for the one(s) that has been around so long that it's become a part of your landscape. Watch out for those demons that seem harmless. You know them. Watch out for that one that you like, that little "pet" demon you have, the one you keep secretly. It's quiet, seems harmless and under control. Watch out especially for that one.

[ddd] Ezekiel 28:12014

The text clearly says there's a sin which easily trips us up. It tells us to strip it off. KJV tells us to lay it aside. If the Bible says to do it, then it's possible to do, if not by will power, then with the help of the Holy Spirit who is always available. If you can lay it aside, then you know what it is. You're familiar with the sin that gets you every time but for some reason you hold

> *Therefore, since we are surrounded by such a huge crowd of witnesses to the life of faith, let us strip off every weight that slows us down,* **especially the sin that so easily trips us up.** *And let us run with endurance the race God has set before us.*
>
> *Hebrews 12:1*

onto it. This is not meant to be a criticism, just a nudge. The sin that so easily trips you up could be something as common as a substance addiction; a bad habit; hanging with a subpar inner circle; an addiction you think you can manage; shopping; competitiveness; or just something you like, that little feel good demon, the pet spoken of earlier. Strip it off, lay it aside,[eee] throw it off.[fff] Whichever translation you choose to use, the imperative is offensive action required on your part to get rid of it. You can't cast it off and take it with you at the same time. Once you've cast it off, then it's behind you; it's in the past. Paul speaks up saying, forget about it, and aggressively move on.[ggg] Know this, a demon is a demon, no matter how subtle, cute, friendly it is or how long it's been with you. It's still a demon.

[eee] KJV
[fff] NIV
[ggg] Philippians 3:14

PRAYERFULLY PONDER

Ponder these thoughts carefully before you respond.

1. Do you have a pet demon?

_____

_____

_____

2. Some demons have become so familiar that you don't mind them being around.

_____

_____

_____

3. Some demons have been around so long that they've become a part of the landscape. Are they harmless?

_____

_____

_____

_____

And we being exceedingly tossed with a tempest, the next day they lightened the ship; And the third day we cast out with our own hands the tackling of the ship.   *Acts 27:18, 19*

THOU SHALL TRAVEL LIGHT

INTRODUCE THE FINAL COMMANDMENT IN THIS book with a personal story. In the early years of my corporate career I traveled quite a lot. I enjoyed every part of it, my work, the flights, seeing new places, meeting new people in various positions in my profession. It was work but each like a mini vacation. I enjoyed every part of it except one, the luggage. I'd invested in beautiful luggage. Packing wasn't the problem; even that was enjoyable. But, in those days, there was no curbside baggage check, moving sidewalks, or indoor shuttles. You checked your bags at the flight gate. Therein was the nightmare; getting my luggage through the airport to the flight gate. My only hope was that there might be one of those motorized passenger cars available; but even those were in short supply and not at every airport. Occasionally someone would feel sorry for me and help me with my luggage but not often.

In an airport one afternoon, I noticed others moving quickly, effortlessly, sitting comfortably at the little snack tables waiting for their flights, while I sat at the gate guarding my luggage, taking up more than my fair share of space. One of my colleagues said, "Your luggage is beautiful but why do you bring so much? You don't need to bring your whole life with you." What an awakening. I honestly thought I needed all of it. I'd become so accustomed to the burdensome luggage that I accepted it as just an unpleasant part of the trips. Believing everything was needed, I never gave a single thought to lightening my load until questioned about it. One seasoned in the position was also a seasoned traveler who knew exactly what they needed for the journey, taking only what they needed.

FIGURE 1 THE ROOKIE TRAVELER

Inexperienced, rookie travelers take more than they need, costing them extra baggage fees at the airport or schlepping heavy bags through train stations. Onlookers shake their heads at the overburdened traveler. Others may lend a hand. Still others may want to help but are struggling to deal with their own luggage.

Jesus understood the advantage of traveling light. In neither of the four Gospel accounts or stories about him, no matter how vivid the imagery, is there ever mention of Jesus carrying luggage. He covered a lot of miles on foot, but never a mention of luggage. Even in the movies he had nothing more than the clothes on his back. So, when he sent his disciples out on assignment telling them to take nothing with them,[hhh], he was asking them to do what he'd always done, travel light. Without tangible things to keep up with, worry about where to store, about getting mugged on the road or robbed when they laid things aside to minister, they would be unencumbered, unrestrained, and free to focus on their mission. That makes perfect sense if you think about it. They could get what they needed when they got where they were going. The less they took, the less the stress and more the time and mental energy available for their assignments. Surely the disciples had the normal life issues that may have caused distraction but that wasn't the subject of Jesus' concern. If there weren't the

---

[hhh] Matthew 10:9-10; Mark 6:8; Luke 9:3

potential hindrance to completing their assignments because of tangible things, then Jesus wouldn't have bothered to tell them to take nothing with them.

The accumulation of things is the norm in a consumerist culture. Too often the volume or expense of one's possession is the measure of their self-worth, judged by themselves and others. Cars, clothes, jewelry, real estate, art, antiques, ... God's world is beautiful and he's put things here to be enjoyed. Things for which to be grateful. **Note to self: It's okay to have things if the things don't have you.** What does that mean, if the things don't have you? It means, the more you desire, the more you acquire; the more you acquire the more is required. Tangible things can almost seem to take on life. They require attention, maintenance, renewal, repair, etc. They come with a cost; bills, mortgages, insurance, warrantees, credit cards, memberships, etc. Things must be paid for. **Note to self: Just because you can buy it doesn't mean you can afford it.** This isn't an admonition to live a life of monasticism unless that's your thing.

The more you desire, the more you acquire. The more you acquire, the more is required.

This is a warning to be conscious of debt. It very subtly becomes your master. Debt will own you and your time. When you have debt and you bow beneath the weight of it, your thoughts are consumed with how to get out from under it. Another way to put it is, you can be a slave to debt. Debt puts limitations on your freedom. Once enslaved to debt, your choices are no longer your own. You can't spend your money or give because you've already spent it, so whatever you get in the future must pay for the past. Too much debt means too much worry. Debt demands overtime, hence, less time for the things of God. Debt is a heavy weight. Beloved, travel light.

Check Your Bags

Imagine at birth being given one empty piece of luggage, a carry-on piece, in which to keep your life experiences. See the instructions on the tag. The purpose of this piece of luggage is to enable you to conveniently keep with you the experiences you need, and lessons learned. The piece of luggage is marked MEMORIES.

1. Keep only what you need.
2. Check bag regularly.
3. Unpack & Dump the things that weigh you down.

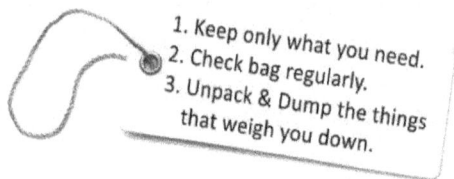

FIGURE 2 DO NOT REMOVE THIS TAG

Although everything goes in, good and bad, you don't need to keep everything. **[Note to self: Some experiences are by choice, so be careful what you pack. The more you pack, the more there is to unpack.]** Things get in your bag in several ways. You put them there (avoidable mistakes; self-inflicted wounds); other things are dumped on you by others via their meanness, cruel words, insecurities, ignorance, whatever. [iii] Other times it's just things that come with living; unemployment, illness, death of a loved one, bad breaks, etc. In the final analysis, it doesn't matter what caused the pain. Pain is pain. Whatever happened, happened. It cannot unhappen. The question is, did you unpack your bags from the experience?

Life is a common experience. To move through life with good strength and agility, you must do maintenance by looking through your luggage, keeping what's good and unpacking what isn't. Good things happen and we find joy and praise God for the good things. Bad things happen, some quite devastating. Good or bad, experiences leave behind residue, and that's what you're looking for, the residue. Yes, all things, good and bad, work together for good,[iii] but, please understand, the "good" is what you've learned from the experience. "What has this experience done to me, or for me? What residue has it left

---

[iii] See the 6th Commandment
[iii] Romans 8:28

behind in my life? The residue left behind is what you decide to keep or discard. Keep what is valuable, praise worthy, life giving, instructive. The rest is garbage. Do what you do with garbage. Discard it. Throw it away.

If you don't unpack, hoarding painful memories, insults, the dregs in the life experience, they'll take up increasingly more space. Instead of discarding the bad stuff you'll add extra luggage to accommodate the load. Now you've officially got baggage! Baggage to drag around everywhere you go, heavy with the vestiges of life's experiences. Look at this poor soul below. Maybe the tag fell off his one piece of carry-on luggage and he never knew to check, unpack and dump. Maybe he thinks that's how life is supposed to be. He continued to add more pieces to hold the memories, until he finally needed a wagon to carry it all. In his wagon, there's no room for joy, hope, or praise for life. Maybe unkind, uncomplimentary words were hurled at him at a young age that shattered his self-esteem making it difficult, if not impossible, to

Unpack or you will preach what's in your bag

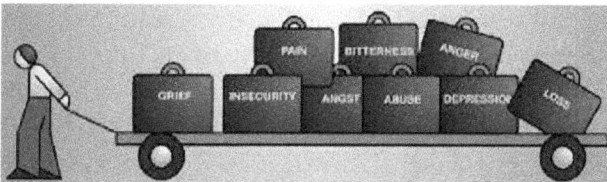

FIGURE 3 DON'T DRAG YOUR BAGGAGE INTO THE PULPIT

believe in himself. Maybe there was no one there to tell him what he heard was untrue. No one to tell him he was fearfully and wonderfully made. [kkk] Maybe he was raised in an environment of criticism, someone asking "Why can't you be like your cousin or the boy down the street?" leaving him insecure.

[kkk] Psalm 139:14

Maybe he got a bad break in a business deal with a friend, and now he's angry. Maybe he's late middle age and he thinks his dreams will never happen and he's bitter and depressed. There's a cliché that says, "Time heals all wounds." Not so. Wounds, hurts, habits, memories, broken dreams, disappointments, bad decisions, regrets, ... become baggage, intangible baggage.

Where's his inner circle? Either he doesn't have one or the inner circle he has does not have the right people in it. If his inner circle was effective they'd say, "We'll help you to throw that stuff off your wagon." There are a lot of good people pulling a wagon like this.

Life, Inc.

Imagine life as a company and you've been hired. Welcome to the company, you're now on the clock. You'll get sick on the job but life offers no sick days. You'll get wounded on the job but life offers no time off for healing. You know the importance of priorities and responsibilities and you want to handle your job in mature and honorable way. Life, however, shows no partiality. You can go about doing everything as right as is humanly possible and suddenly life throws a curve ball or decks you with a sucker punch. You didn't see it coming. You didn't deserve it. You didn't cause it. You've been hurt. You've been assaulted by life but there's no time to deal with it. Who's got time to stop and nurse their wounds. Life keeps moving even when you slow down or stop. You heal on the go, so to speak. You say to yourself, "I'll be okay." And for the most part you may be okay because you're awesome and you can function, so you shake yourself, close your bag, ignore it, feel strong and move on (so you hope or so you may think)? Unless you intentionally check your bags from time to time, unpack and dump the garbage, it stays with you. You can fake being strong but people will see your baggage and smell your garbage

You may need help unpacking. Nothing wrong with that. You may feel alone but you aren't. That's one reason the whole Fourth Commandment is about your inner circle and their value in your life. Your inner circle isn't just a group of friends who conveniently hang out together. Your inner circle has purpose; to help you get to your purpose. Say it with me again. Life happens. Everyone accumulates baggage but you don't have to keep it.

Lighten Your Load Before the Storm

In Acts 27, Paul was a prisoner being taken by sea to Rome, Italy, to appear before the court of Caesar. During the trip a fierce nor'easter arose threatening the lives of everyone on board and destruction of the ship. The men did two things to lighten the load to save the ship. First, they threw cargo overboard. Second, they threw the ship's equipment overboard. Everything they threw overboard was considered important enough to carry onboard, but when the storm hit and their lives were threatened, they threw those things overboard.

Don't wait until there's a storm in your life to lighten your load. Travel light.

There is No Recall of the Call

Guess what, preacher. The call to preach doesn't exempt or shield you from life events that cripples the human soul. There's no recall of the call. The preacher is expected to do what he or she has been called to do; expected to leave their baggage at the altar like the laity are encouraged to do, or at the very least, leave it outside. No one wants to see the preacher's baggage, except the gossipers and nay sayers, who seek fodder to use as fiery darts. "If you're all burdened down, how can you help me?" "If you're falling apart, how can you tell me Christ will do for me what he's not doing for you?" A broken, insecure person with unhealed wounds in their baggage cannot be a servant because they will use and abuse the people of God trying to meet their own needs. You have the same needs as anyone else but you don't have the right to have your needs met at the expense of the people you're called to serve. You're expected to have it all together in Christ, and do what you're called to do. How is that possible? It's possible because you can do all things through Christ who strengthens you.[lll] This isn't to deny the humanity of the preacher or the reality of pain and the lifelong threat to wellbeing that some experiences cause. On the contrary, this commandment is to affirm that life lands crushing blows, the effects of which can haunt for a lifetime if left in your life bag. It's saying your calling expects you to subject your humanity to the Holy Spirit. Lean on everything you have at your disposal; prayer, the Word, the Holy Spirit, your inner circle, even vacation time, to get up on your feet and walk in the power of God before the people of God. If you're a pastor, you've got to show up every Sunday and step to the mic. No matter in what capacity you serve, you've got to show up strong.[mmm] Do your spiritual due diligence, check your bags regularly so you can show up correct.

Finally, being confident of this very thing. He who has begun a good work in you will perform it until the day of Jesus Christ.

PS I introduced the final commandment of this book with a story of how in the early days of my corporate career I travelled with far too much luggage. Well, I finally got it. Travel came with the position and how I traveled reflected my level of professional maturity. I learned to travel light.

[lll] Philippians 4:13
[mmm] II Chronicles 16:9

PRAYERFULLY PONDER

What's in Your Bag?

Unpack or you'll preach what's in your bag

1. Do you have unresolved issues from your past that follow you into the pulpit? Circle each that applies or write your own.

- Are you angry with anyone?
- Did someone betray you in a relationship or business?
- Do you have an issue of unforgiveness?

_____

_____

2. Are you wrestling with insecurities? Yes _____ No _____

3. Is there anyone in your inner circle and/or outer circle who shouldn't be there? Yes _____ No _____

4. Are there any habits in your baggage that shouldn't be there?

Yes _____ No _____

5. Do you have a "soapbox" sermon?

THE TEN COMMANDMENTS OF PREACHING

1st	THOU SHALL KEEP THY HEAD ON STRAIGHT	Regularly check for the EGW virus
2nd	THOU SHALL BE THINE AUTHENTIC SELF	Be not guilty of "Identity Theft"
3rd	THOU SHALL LINK TO THE CLOUD	Make prayer your Homepage
4th	THOU SHALL WISELY CHOOSE THY INNER CIRCLE	You are the average of the five people with whom you spend the most time
5th	THOU SHALL FLEE JEALOUSY & ENVY	You can be a victim or an offender
6th	THOU SHALL NOT KILL	Watch your mouth!
7th	THOU SHALL DO THY HOMEWORK THOROUGHLY	Be the standard bearer for excellence
8th	THOU SHALL NOT STEAL	Be a person of integrity. Don't steal. Give credit.
9th	THOU SHALL KNOW THY DEMONS	They know you!
10th	THOU SHALL TRAVEL LIGHT	Check your bags regularly. Unpack regularly. Keep only what you need.

Notes

ABOUT THE AUTHOR

CL LAWRENCE, LEADERSHIP DEVELOPMENT STRATEGIST, a dynamic Christian communicator best known for her eclectic approach to teaching and preaching the Word of God and distinctive gift of discovering contemporary insights in the Biblical stories while maintaining the integrity of the Biblical text. Her passion for excellence has made her a much sought after conference speaker, seminar facilitator. Exciting. Thought provoking. Empowering, are words used to describe her ministry "Boot Camps," and other events. She combines a 12-year tenure in Corporate America with 30+ years of pastoral and church leadership.

A graduate of Cheyney University, Lutheran Theological Seminary and Tony Campolo School for Social Change, Carol is the founder of Lawrence Seminars, Inc., Host of Empowerment Gatherings (worship/ networking events); and Teacher/Facilitator of "Women at the Well" (a unique approach to Bible Study for Women Only). A.K.A. "ZseZse," she's the Creator, Host and Producer of the podcast "Jazz Divine; Zse-votions, (devotional CDs); and the Blogcast, "Just Thinking."

To book an engagement
Email:
DrL@LawrenceMinistries.com
Visit:
LawrenceMinistries.com

******** 2017 ********

LOOK FOR THESE & OTHER TITLES ON AMAZON.COM & KINDLE.COM

VICTORY OVER YOUR ENEMY
THE JEHOSHAPHAT SAGA
(II CHRONICLES 20)

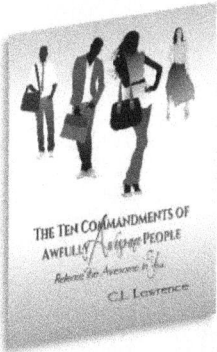

THE TEN COMMANDMENTS
OF AWFULLY AWESOME PEOPLE
RELEASE THE AWESOME IN YOU!

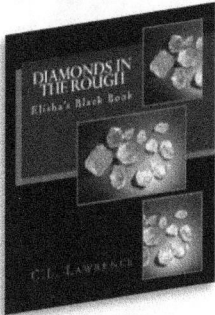

DIAMONDS IN THE ROUGH
ELISHA'S PLAYBOOK
FOR ASSOCIATE MINISTERS

www.ingramcontent.com/pod-product-compliance
Lightning Source LLC
Chambersburg PA
CBHW021155020426
42331CB00003B/63